The Sacred Sword

Teachings of the Psychic Channel

Betty Bethards

▲

Edited and with Commentary by

Cary Odom

THE INNER LIGHT FOUNDATION
P. O. Box 761
Novato, California   94947

This book
is dedicated to my son

Wayne

who "crossed over" to the other side
on January 12, 1971

And my deep appreciation
is expressed to all who helped
make this book possible,
whether they may be in or out
of the body

— Betty Bethards

PREFACE

The teachings of *The Sacred Sword* take you on a journey to the depths of your own being. Along the way you encounter signposts—karma, reincarnation, death, psychic phenomena, peace, personal growth, meditation.

Is the journey unorthodox? That depends on your present perspective. Is it helpful? Many persons have found their lives transformed. Is it believable? "Practice the teachings and decide for yourself."

This is the counsel of Betty Bethards, the psychic channel who helps point the way.

CONTENTS

Chapter One

INTRODUCTION

A Guest in the Kitchen

Let's say you have a good friend who has just died. And then about a week from now this person shows up in your kitchen. What would *you* do?

This was the plight of Betty Bethards, middle class wife and mother, who enjoyed the normal, ordinary things in life. She was twenty-two at the time, had been married for six years, had two children, and was devoted to bridge and bowling.

She was wandering around her kitchen one day, washing a few dishes and putting away odds and ends. Suddenly she had a cold chill down her spine. She looked up and saw Jerry.

1

Betty had attended Jerry's funeral no more than a week ago.

"Go away, you're dead!" she cried out. But he remained, hovering several feet off the floor in a body and clothes just as Betty had last remembered him.

"I'm not leaving until you take a message to my wife," explained Jerry, communicating with Betty through telepathy.

"I must be imagining things," she tried to assure herself. After all, being raised a fundamentalist Baptist (later turned Methodist) she believed that "when you died you were put in the ground and stayed there—at least until the final judgment day." Maybe Jerry had other ideas. But she didn't want any part of it.

Still, Jerry insisted upon staying until Betty agreed to write down specific details concerning the handling of his unfinished business affairs. In the process Betty asked ten questions of her own, and recorded his responses.

Finally she got down all the information, and, as instructed, sent it to Jerry's wife who was now in another city. She felt rather silly and apologetic. But after all, she couldn't go on entertaining Jerry in her kitchen forever, could she?

About a week later she got a letter back: "Betty, I don't know how you did it, but you must have been in touch with Jerry. Your letter answered all the questions about handling final details. Everything checked out. Once again I know all is well."

After that Jerry disappeared, and Betty never saw him again. Yet during the course of the week she had reflected many times on the events surrounding his "death." She had felt an overwhelming urge the night of his passing to go to the hospital. She had left in the middle of preparing dinner, her husband angrily trying to prevent her from going. She had arrived at the hospital just in time to be with his wife after the doctors had pronounced him dead.

Then Betty remembered the funeral itself. She had never seen a corpse before, and was afraid to go to the funeral home. She realized that she would have to hold up, to give strength to Jerry's wife. So she went to the mortuary before anyone else to view the body. After inching her way across the room, she peered into the casket.

"That's not Jerry," she thought. "That's an empty shell." She was no longer afraid and she started looking around the room for him. Now where did she get such an idea? She hadn't remembered all these things when Jerry had first made his appearance in her kitchen. But somehow she had been subtly prepared for what was to follow.

APPROACHING THE CROSSROADS

During the next ten years, Betty began to have dreams about various happenings—and they usually came true. For the most part they were about her friends, and sometimes she would relate them. Some were dreams of accidents and tragedies. And her friends began to say to her, "Hey, Betty, do me a favor and don't dream about me tonight."

During this same ten year period she went through a divorce, remarried, and had two more children. She remained an avid bridge player and bowler, and in addition became extremely fond of working jigsaw puzzles.

The family moved around a lot before finally settling down in Novato, California. Right before moving to Novato in 1967, they lived in Bellevue, Washington. It was here that Betty, now at age 32, was approaching a major crossroads in her life. One night she returned home from a bridge game, and felt a slight burning sensation in her chest. She went to bed. An hour later she awoke to find herself hovering over the bed, about two feet from her own body. A voice was saying, "You're going to have pneumonia. Get to a doctor."

Betty was frantic. "I was so scared I literally pulled myself back into my body again." Almost in tears, she woke up her husband.

"I was floating above my body," she blurted out.

"That's okay, honey," he answered sleepily. "It'll be all right in the morning."

But the next day Betty insisted that she be taken to a physician. The first doctor announced that she was fine, and said for her to go home and take aspirin. She then went to an internist, told him she had pneumonia, and demanded a chest X-ray.

"Lady, you haven't got pneumonia," said the internist, "but it's your fourteen dollars."

Sure enough, the X-ray showed pneumonia beginning in the left lung. Again, the prescription was to go home and rest—no antibiotics were given.

For the next two weeks Betty had temperatures of 103-104 degrees, and she grew weaker and weaker. At the end of that period she found herself sitting on her couch, with hardly enough energy to move.

Suddenly "she" was twenty feet across the room. "Everything I considered Betty to be— memory, personality, senses—was looking back at that shell on the couch. I thought, 'Gee, she's sick. I don't want to go back.' And a very gentle voice behind me said, 'You don't have to go back. But this is death if you choose to stay.' "

Betty looked at her "new" self. "I had a body which appeared the same, had the same clothes on it, and was raised about two feet off the floor. I wasn't frightened at all, because I felt wonderful. It was beautiful."

She then understood how Jerry had come to her. "It was all so clear. I knew then that there is no such thing as death."

THE DECISION

But she found herself thinking about her children. "What if the kids come in and find me sitting there? They'll start crying. They won't know I haven't gone any place." At that point she made her decision. "I can't leave my thirteen-month-old son, for he still needs me," she thought.

The voice returned: "Unless you take an antibiotic within the next twenty-four hours, you will no longer have a choice of whether you wish to remain on the earth plane." At that moment she found herself back in the body on the couch.

As soon as her husband came home, she told him she had to have the antibiotic. They found a doctor, got the medication, and the fever broke almost immediately. It took about a year for her energy level to return to normal.

THE SEARCH FOR UNDERSTANDING

Her experiences across the next several years

continued to be dramatic, and they were marked by tremendous personal struggle and doubt. Betty began to develop automatic writing, which she considered unreliable. This led her into the beginning stages of mediumship.

She heard voices, and felt she was in touch with spirit guides around her. But she remained a skeptic. Was she going nuts ? She went to ministers and doctors asking for help. Finally, her own minister counseled, "Betty, as long as what is being told you is good, there seems to be no harm in continuing. Pray for guidance, and ask God how to understand what is happening."

Betty was spending many frustrating nights following the directions of these inner teachers, and she was rapidly developing her mediumship and increasing her general psychic sensitivity. Sometimes she would spend four or five hours a night working with her spirit guides, mainly because her husband insisted that she do this. If the teachings are good she must follow them, he persuaded her. And Betty would have stopped if it hadn't been for this constant urging.

The different spirit teachers would come and go, and this was upsetting and confusing. Finally, after many months of trying to understand what all this might mean, Betty had reached a point where she felt she couldn't go on. She told her husband that she was going to give the whole thing up. "Maybe it's just my imagination," she said.

"That's okay, dear. But I'm not going to stop trying to listen. I've got to go on," he replied.

"How can he?" thought Betty. "He doesn't hear anything or see anything. How can he go on without me?"

So Betty prayed for four days, asking that she be told, once and for all, what this was all about, and how to understand the voices, the instructions, and the visions. "I've got to have a sign that this isn't just in Betty's head," she said, "or I'll quit."

THE SIGN AT LAST

At the end of the four days her husband joined her, and they continued in silence together. Then there was a sudden rush of energy into the room, and Betty was levitated off the floor.

"Oh, God," she thought, "they're going to drop me on my nose!" But "they" didn't and she floated gently down. She wanted a sign— and she got one. After that she was taught a simple meditation technique, a way for her to control her psychic and spiritual development. Several days later her primary spirit guide, a Peruvian Indian named Uvalla, came and identified himself. He has been with Betty ever since.

Today she is known to thousands of people as the "psychic channel Betty Bethards." This means, first of all, that she has psychic ability— she is clairvoyant, clairaudient, and clairsentient. Secondly, she is able to receive information from sources beyond ordinary human knowledge. She channels through information from her spirit teachers.

Betty was told that she would be working as both healer and teacher, that she would establish a foundation, work with psychical researchers, and lecture to many audiences. These things, of course, she has done and continues to do. Numerous articles have been published about her, and she has been featured on television and radio programs. She recently completed a series on meditation for an educational television network.

THE HEART OF THE MESSAGE

But what actually are these teachings she has received? What is her message?

In short, the teachings emphasize personal responsibility. You are accountable for your every thought, every word, and every action. Your purpose here on earth is to grow in understanding, in knowledge, and in love.

The message is rooted in a philosophy foreign to Betty's initial upbringing—the idea that you can't learn everything in one lifetime. So you are given many lifetimes, in many different situations. This is the principle of reincarnation.

Reincarnation occurs mainly because we don't learn our lessons, and because we are bound by an unalterable law of the universe—the law of karma. Karma is the principle of cause and effect that extends throughout our many lifetimes: as we sow, we reap.

From ancient traditions, this karmic power has been symbolized by a two-edged sword. It is a reciprocating power. It cuts both ways. If we radiate love, we receive love. If we radiate peace, we receive peace. But if the sword is wielded in an unthinking, unloving manner, the very body it scars is that of the wielder. It can be dangerous and destructive, or it can point the way to ultimate freedom.

Karma, then, represents a power entrusted to each one of us to use according to our own wills. But, say Betty's teachers, we have forgotten that this sword, this power, is sacred. We have forgotten that it is to be used for creating a world of peace, not a world of discord.

Betty's message calls for us to remember the sacred sword. For it represents the just, the beautiful, the magnificent law of the cosmos. And to survive in an age of great sorrow and disillusionment, the sword must be recognized— the law understood—and hallowed once again by mankind.

More of what it's all about will be found in the following pages. Seems fantastic? "Yes, it is," grins Betty. "Life is more than I ever imagined. All I want to do is learn. There is so much to know."

Chapter Two

UNDERSTANDING BETTY: PERSON VERSUS CHANNEL

The personality of Betty Bethards is one thing. The spirit guides who speak through her "channel" are something else.

What actually is a "channel"? It may be considered a passageway or vehicle through which something flows. Or, it may be a narrow band of frequencies which conveys a single radio or television communication. In Betty's case, we might say she is a vehicle, operating as a receiving station. She is using high frequencies in her consciousness to *tune in—to bring through*—a channel that most of us don't ordinarily see or hear.

She is told that she should strive continuously to develop a "higher channel"—that is, continue raising her own vibrations or frequencies so that she can pick up finer and subtler energies.

When she brings through information, she describes herself as "once removed" from what is being said. "I hear me," she explains, "but it's as if I am able to suspend the working of my conscious mind so that another dimension is able to function. It takes a good deal of concentration, which I probably developed from working so many jigsaw puzzles."

Betty the personality considers herself a student of Betty the channel. She maintains a healthy skepticism, though, about the things which come through: "No channel is going to be 100 per cent accurate." Her counsel to herself, and to others, is to "take what feels right, and put the rest aside. You may go back and pick it up later, or you may find that it isn't right for your life."

Why has she come to trust what she receives as fully as she does? Mostly for pragmatic reasons. Over the last four and a half years she has "read" for hundreds of people—picking up information which helps provide solutions to their problems. People feel renewed and encouraged from their encounters with her.

She has seen the meditation technique revolutionize many lives, including her own. "It works," she says, "Meditation really works.

The teachings are elaborations of what you learn through your own meditation practice."

In this chapter Betty's spirit guides are questioned on how they actually operate, who they are, the nature of the channel, and how to understand Betty's "gift." (They are speaking through Betty.)

HOW WOULD YOU DESCRIBE THE DIFFERENCE
BETWEEN BETTY THE PERSON AND
BETTY THE CHANNEL?

Betty the person has access to knowledge which is in the subconscious and conscious mind. She has access to information through personal experience, reading, and to that which she is open to receive from the channel.

We who speak through the channel have access to the many realms of knowledge. But nothing can be given unless she is ready to receive it. We cannot tell Betty how to make decisions or how to live her life. We bring through the teachings, and she must try to live up to these. She must try to understand the channel, try to purify her own thoughts.

YOU SEEM TO EXPLAIN THE DIFFERENCE
IN TERMS OF AWARENESS.

Each entity is defined in terms of its own awareness. Your concept of reality, your

personality, hinge on the purity of your
perceptions. Entities are known on our realm
by their degree of spiritual knowledge, or
unfoldment.

OFTEN YOU HAVE CALLED BETTY A
"CHANNEL OF LOVE."

This is her whole emphasis. She radiates
through the heart chakra the power she receives
from the channel. This is the vibration of love.
[*Note: A "chakra" is an energy center.*]

WHAT IS A "CHANNEL"?

It is an energy beam or wave of light. The
higher the frequency, the more developed a
person must be to receive it. You must be able
to process a great amount of current or energy
through your body to pick up the higher
channels. The ability to process this energy
is gained through meditation.

WOULD YOU DISCUSS BETTY'S
"PSYCHIC MEDIUMSHIP"?

Strictly speaking she could not be called a
medium. Her ability differs from straight
mediumship in that she is still *aware* when
we speak through her. It is not necessary for
her to go into a deep trance and give up
control in order to receive. But she *can* do this,
and has on occasion.

She has an intuitional ability far above the average person. She could be called clairsentient—which means she can feel or sense with an unusual degree of perception. This sensitivity reaches beyond the astral plane and is superior to psychic abilities which originate there.

She does, however, have what you would call clairvoyance and clairaudience. Her ability to know events in both past and future comes from her channel.

DIDN'T ALL THESE "ABILITIES" COME ON RATHER SUDDENLY?

It is true she has been in a rapid training session the last four and a half years. During this incarnation she has always manifested some of this ability, although it was not nearly so pronounced.

WHAT ARE BETTY'S TASKS IN THIS NEW ROLE?

She is a teacher. Her task is to channel through the mystical teachings in simple language that people will readily understand. These teachings are adaptable to an individual's level of awareness. And a key word in the teachings is *awareness*—we want you to grow in awareness of the inner self, in awareness of

the love which can radiate from the inner self
to all souls.

WHAT ABOUT HER WORK AS HEALER?

You cannot separate the healing from the
teaching. She is teaching people to heal their
own spiritual vehicles. Every man has the tools
with which to do this—she merely points to
these tools. The healing is what she's teaching—
how man can bring into harmony his own vibrations, and thus attune himself to the God center
of his being.

HOW WOULD YOU IDENTIFY YOURSELVES AS SPIRIT GUIDES?

We are members of an organization called
the White Brotherhood. White means *light*, and
has nothing to do with race. The White
Brotherhood have been members of every race,
and know only the oneness of the *human* race.

We are teachers who have worked with Jesus
and many other masters. Our main purpose is
to enlighten man, to help him realize his full
potential.

It is not necessary to know our names. But
for ease in communication, Betty felt it
important to know her main guide. This is
Uvalla, a Peruvian teacher, who is out of the
body and will not incarnate again on the earth
plane.

HOW ARE WE TO KNOW WHICH
OF THE TEACHINGS ARE TRUE, AND
WHICH ARE COLORED BY THE PERSONALITY?

It is impossible for anyone in the human body to receive clear impressions all the time. Take that which is comfortable, that which you can accept, and put the remainder away. A soul will hear only what it is ready to hear.

Betty still does not agree with many of the things which come through her, and this is fine. Other people, however, might feel perfectly comfortable with the same information. When you are ready, something within you will say, "I know that." Truth lies within your own soul. You might pass a beggar on the street, and he could give you a truth as profound as that which would come from a spiritual leader. Truth is within everyone, and comes in many forms.

WHAT ACTUALLY IS TRUTH?

Truth corresponds with the level of vibration that is the highest in the universe. Truth reflects the permeating energy which is behind all manifested reality. Truth is understood on various levels, depending on the awareness of the entity. How can we explain the abstraction of truth? It is like a preface to God.

An entity which is picking up something that is "true" about another may be reading it from any of the several planes. The *higher* the plane he taps, the stronger the perception, and the more nearly correct the information.

▲

Betty often feels the weight of responsibility in the dual role of person and channel. Her guides explain that "she chose to assume the responsibility of the teachings before incarnating, and she is working to fulfill that which she came back to do. Although she complains a great deal about it, she will carry on." ("If I knew how to get in touch with God, I'd resign" is one of Betty's favorite expressions.)

Chapter Three

KARMA AND REINCARNATION

The interwoven concepts of karma and re-incarnation have been known in both Eastern and Western worlds from ancient times. And some historians claim these ideas once had wide acceptance in the early Christian Church.

But they have remained hidden from the "average American" of today until very recently. Students have been exposed to these concepts through the academic study of world religions, but for the most part the audience has been limited.

Perhaps the most significant factor in the re-discovery of karma and reincarnation has been the work of the American psychic Edgar Cayce. In the last twenty years, books about his life and teachings have reached a peak of popularity—

and the "average American" has begun to read about, and to take seriously, the possibility of karma and reincarnation. (Of course, there are now many books on the market dealing with these ideas in a variety of ways.)

Betty, like Cayce, had a conservative Protestant Christian background. When teachings about karma and reincarnation began to come through her, she was confused and unbelieving. But as these concepts became more and more central in the emerging teaching, she knew she would have to come to terms with them.

In essence the ideas are easy enough to understand. Reincarnation suggests that a person is basically spirit or consciousness which takes on bodily form, and is born into lifetime after lifetime. Literally it means "spirit becoming flesh again and again."

Karma refers to the law or principle which governs what one experiences in his various lifetimes. Sometimes it is called the "cosmic law of cause and effect." Most simply, it means that our thoughts and deeds have consequences—not only in this lifetime, but in future existences as well.

In response to questioning, Betty's spirit guides have spoken through her at length on these topics.

WHAT IS REINCARNATION?

It is a natural, normal process of the evolution, or development, of the soul. The process provides the soul the opportunity to struggle, to grow, and to learn. The soul is able gradually to raise its level of vibration, so that it may enter new dimensions of being.

THIS PROCESS DOESN'T GO ON FOREVER, THEN?

Certainly not. The whole purpose of the soul's existence on the earth plane is to free itself from the necessity of endless rebirths. Each self chooses how fast he wishes to progress.

YOU SPEAK OF PURPOSE. DOES THIS MEAN THERE IS SOME KIND OF PLAN OR PURPOSE FOR EVERYONE?

You could say that the Universal Mind, or God, has a plan for his creatures, yes. Ultimately it is that they should be united with Him. This is a kind of master plan for everyone. You know from your very first incarnation that your task is to find your way to the infinite love-power of the universe, to God.

BUT IS THERE A "PLAN" FOR EACH INDIVIDUAL LIFETIME?

Not a plan imposed from without. One way of saying it is that God, through the spirit entities who are his agents, helps you work out a plan before each incarnation. Although you receive help, it is your own choice. So before each soul incarnates on the earth plane, it plans carefully what it hopes to accomplish in that lifetime. It decides what strengths or weaknesses it desires to unfold and learn to control. It decides what karma it wishes to work out.

YOU MENTION KARMA—EXACTLY WHAT DO YOU MEAN?

Karma simply means you will harvest exactly what you have planted. It is the principle of individual responsibility. You control your own destiny by your thoughts, words, and deeds. The Western world is familiar with the idea, not linked with the concept of reincarnation, through the words of St. Paul: "Whatsoever a man soweth, that shall he also reap."

DOES THIS MEAN THAT WE ARE PREDESTINED?

In an ultimate sense you are. Each soul is predestined eventually to return to its spiritual home in the infinite reality. But what is to happen to you in any particular lifetime is predetermined only by your own freely-chosen deeds—by your own choices in this or previous existences.

HOW DO WE KNOW WHAT WE CHOSE FOR OUR PRESENT LIFE?

Memory is largely erased at birth, but the spiritually developed person may see his prior lifetimes. Some psychics can see the previous lifetimes of others. But everyone can know that he chose the circumstances of his present life— his parents, his nationality, his race, the astrological signs under which he enters the earth plane. And everyone can know that his task is to *grow*, to develop the quality of love and to acquire fuller spiritual understanding. What you are experiencing is what you chose.

Once you understand that you intentionally selected your present existence, you are able to ask *why* you selected these circumstances. There is always a reason. Was your childhood unhappy? Perhaps you hurt your parents in a past life, and this is now your karma, or the result of your actions.

As you come to understand it, you will see that this impersonal law of karma, which may look harsh and uncaring, is wondrously kind. It is not punishment, but *opportunity*. It provides a fresh chance to correct past mistakes and continue your evolution toward your ultimate goal.

THEN IN A REAL SENSE, EVEN
THE SUFFERING LIFE BRINGS IS
ACTUALLY AN OPPORTUNITY?

That is exactly right. Your suffering is your opportunity. For example, if you blame your parents for your unhappiness, you can be sure there is karma to be worked out. You will meet them again and again until you can feel compassion and love. In this way every relationship in every incarnation is an opportunity to grow —an opportunity for which you should be thankful.

WOULD YOU COMMENT FURTHER ON
CHOOSING OUR RACE?

Yes, if people could realize this there would be no racial prejudice. Each person would see every other person as a fellow entity working out his karma in his particular situation. Each would support the other in caring and compassion.

People who are prejudiced must return under the same circumstances as those they are critical of. Do you think the soul has race? It is neither yellow, black, red, brown, nor white. All partake of the God nature, and if one hurts another he is really hurting himself.

WHAT ABOUT ADOPTED CHILDREN— WHICH PARENTS HAVE THEY CHOSEN?

The entity has chosen the parents or persons who will be raising it. The natural parents are really unimportant. One is choosing relationships; hence there is no such thing as an "adopted" child. Many heartaches could be avoided if people understood this.

HOW DO THE SEX ROLES RELATE TO REINCARNATION AND KARMA?

First, clearly understand that a spirit has no gender, is neither male nor female. When you come into bodily form, you choose the male or female body depending on what you lack. If, for example, you need to develop the tenderness and love of the mother, you would choose the female body.

Each person has had many incarnations both as man and as woman. You need to learn to see your fellows not as male or female, but as evolving spirits. See yourself the same way—you are only temporarily, for this lifetime, a man or a woman. This is not your permanent identification.

Lesbians and homosexuals lack a clear understanding of their choice of sex role for their present incarnation. They should not feel guilty nor be condemned. Like everyone else, they should try to discover what they intended to learn by having chosen the male or female condition for this lifetime.

YOU SAID THAT ULTIMATELY WE ARE "PREDETERMINED." WOULD YOU SAY MORE ABOUT THE NATURE OF MAN'S WILL IN RELATION TO THIS?

Reincarnation is the means by which each soul is able to learn through experience the lessons it needs in order to work its way to God. There is complete freedom of the will within this process. There is never any coercion from without. Each person chooses his *pace*—how rapidly or slowly he will progress. Each person chooses his *circumstances*—how and when and where he will work out his karma. Each person chooses his *actions*—his specific deeds, attitudes and responses in the various relationships of life.

If one chooses to be vindictive, he reaps the results, or karmic consequences, that vindictiveness produces. If he chooses to be loving, he reaps accordingly. He may choose his actions, but *he cannot choose whether the inevitable consequences will occur.* Another way of saying it is that a person may choose his actions, but not the fruit of his actions.

WHAT ARE THE LIMITS OF FREE WILL?

Theoretically there are no limitations. You are always completely free to decide how you will respond to the situation in which you find yourself. And that situation is itself a result of your karma, or freely chosen deeds.

Practically, there are certain restrictions or impossibilities rooted in the nature of reality. You are a child of God, and you may choose not to behave as a child of God. But you cannot choose not to *be* a child of God. Once you choose a framework or the particular circumstances for a lifetime, you are restricted to operating within that framework. (For example, if you incarnate in a yellow-skinned body you cannot suddenly decide you would like to be brown.) But within your framework you have all the freedom you need, and far more than you can use, for progressing in your life task of growth.

WHAT EXACTLY IS THE WILL?

The will is the entity's directional force. It is the power of will which enables each person to direct his life, to make his choices. The will represents an individual's *strength*. It is his developing ability to select wisely his pathway of growth, to carry out the intent of his life plan. The will goes with one from incarnation to incarnation. It represents what the entity has learned, or earned, in past lifetimes. It is one's developing awareness of purpose, the "steering mechanism" that keeps him pointing forward.

Add "will" to reincarnation and karma and you will have the basic ingredients of the soul's pathway to the infinite. Will is the determination to persevere in the process of working out one's karma through numerous rebirths.

THROUGH SOME OF BETTY'S READINGS
SHE HAS INDICATED THAT PERSONS HAVE
LIVED ON OTHER PLANETS. WHAT ABOUT
KARMA AND REINCARNATION IN RELATION
TO LIFE ON OTHER PLANETS?

The cosmos is alive. There are multitudinous life forms throughout, and the law of karma holds throughout. There are life vibrations on all the planets in your solar system. But the solar system you know is but a dot in infinity. Where an entity resides is limited by his own vibrational rate. He may learn and grow in other spheres when he is ready and when he chooses to do so.

Whether the entity is on the earth, astral, or other planes, he is responsible for his thoughts and deeds. Karma must be paid off on the plane where it is collected.

▲

TEACHING ON REINCARNATION AND KARMA

[*Note: The following is "channeling" which Betty did on reincarnation and karma. She was not in a deep "trance," but was interpreting the teachings of her guides.*]

It is important to realize that your only purpose in incarnating is to grow, to meet responsibilities, and to make decisions. If someone were deciding for you, you would lose the ability to gain insight through your own choices.

Every situation you find yourself in has a lesson for you. If you blame others for your circumstances, you will have to go through these tests again and again until you learn to ask: "What am I to learn from this?" In this way you regard every event as an opportunity for your soul to develop understanding. If you did not make mistakes, there would be no need to incarnate at all. If you did not suffer, you would not learn how to care about your brothers' suffering. Once you've learned a lesson, you will give love and understanding to others who are going through a similar experience.

You must not judge and criticize your fellow man. Each person is on his own level of evolution. Each has his own tasks for this particular lifetime.

Your thoughts as well as your words are heard not only by you and by God, but also by other

entities who may be observing you. When you
realize this, you will change your way of thinking
in a hurry. These entities are there to assist you
much as you yourself might help a friend. They
will not do your growing for you, but they will
support you and share their insights when you
learn how to listen to them. You may call them
your spirit guides or spirit teachers. They
come and go according to your needs.

In addition, each person has one particular
guide who walks with him from the time of
birth to the time of death—throughout his whole
incarnation. This entity is sometimes called one's
guardian angel. It is the job of the guardian
angel to hand out your karma, both good and
bad, and to record the gains and losses of your
soul.

Some people become embittered and lose faith
when they see others taking advantage of their
fellows and seemingly not suffering for their
behavior at all. Don't be angry or bitter! Try to
feel compassion toward such persons, for you
may be sure they will pay for every hurt they
have brought to others. When their suffering
comes, they will likely ask why God has brought
this suffering to them. God did not bring it, of
course—they have done this to themselves, and
they are experiencing their karma. God is love!
He is not a stern figure handing out punishment
as so many of you have been taught.

Love is the strongest force in the universe. It can dissolve all negativity and ignorance. It is the God force. You tune into it when you do that which is loving and kindly, and reject the negative and hostile. It is important to grasp every opportunity to do good and to build constructive attitudes and habits. Petty gossip and criticism of others creates more negative karma than you ever imagine. It holds back your soul's progress because it cuts you off from the love force.

Each entity is free at every moment to reach out and grasp the love power, to call upon it, to realize it within himself. Although it can be tapped at any time, at any place, and in any circumstance, the best way is through meditation.

The wisdom of the universe is within you, waiting to be uncovered. The key is love. Each must sooner or later find the "love way" if he is to "grow back to God" and leave reincarnation behind. If it is not to be done in this lifetime, it will have to be done in a future incarnation. The choice is yours, for you have free will!

Chapter Four

THE NATURE
OF DEATH

Many of the old tabus are being lifted—on
sex, on divorce, on religion. But one primary
tabu still remains: "Don't talk about death!"
The doctor, the minister, the family, the friends
of the dying—all stumble around in confusion.

"Gee, I don't know what to say."

"I wish there were something I could do."

"Make sure you don't let on to grandma she's
dying."

"Why did such a tragic accident have to
happen to John?"

"Death is so final!"

"Death," says Betty, "is just a natural part—
and a potentially beautiful part—of the whole

evolutionary process. Once you have had an out-of-the-body experience, and looked back on your physical shell, you could never doubt the reality of eternal life."

Only comparatively recently scientists have decided that matter and energy are merely different vibratory rates, that energy is never destroyed, only changed or transformed.

Does this mean the energy force which expresses itself in the human being can never be destroyed? Perhaps it goes through various levels of vibration, and the higher levels cannot be seen within the limited visual spectrum of physical eyes—just as the eyes cannot see X-rays or radio waves.

As we learn to think in terms of energy—that all manifested things are representations of diverse vibratory rates—the concept of eternal life begins to take on new meaning.

The following is a combination of two trances on death.

UNDERSTANDING DEATH

Life is eternal. There is no "death." If people could only correctly understand death, they would no longer have any fear of the unknown.

When the soul has chosen to incarnate into physical matter on the earth plane, it is first fed and nourished through an umbilical cord in the womb of the mother. It is also through this cord that the life force is sent to the child.

When it is time for the child to be born and he or she leaves the body of the mother, the cord must be severed. The soul is then fully released into the physical matter of the child, and he must struggle on his own as an individual entity.

He is met with earthly temptations, primarily those concerning whether he will be selfish or loving toward his fellow man. These experiences help him to attain the knowledge and understanding he needs in order to move toward his ultimate spiritual destiny.

When he has been exposed to the opportunities which he chose for the particular lifetime, and has completed his tests, he is allowed a release from the physical body. The soul within knows when the time for release has come.

The so-called "death," which so many misunderstand, is merely a heightening of vibrations. The entity severs himself from the physical body in much the same way as he was severed from his mother's womb.

The invisible cord which connects the entity to the physical body is sometimes called the "silver cord." This silver cord falls away or disconnects as the spirit or entity leaves the body. The personality characteristics, all memories, and all knowledge gained while in the physical form are taken along with the entity.

The only real *change* at death is a freedom of the spirit from the dense matter of the earth plane. The spirit experiences a sensation of release, of heightened awareness, of freedom from all restrictions. Those left behind are, of course, no longer able to communicate with the person on the physical level as before. And they are left with the necessity of disposing of the cast-off body. This they frequently mistake for the entity (person) who formerly wore it.

The entity itself is met by many souls—loved ones, friends, teachers, and guides—as soon as it leaves the earth plane and crosses-over into the spirit realm. As it adapts to the higher realms, it will receive instruction. This then, is the time one will begin to have a better understanding of *self*, and of one's place in the universe.

As one is ready, and as he chooses, he will be shown his past lives. For he must learn to understand the self in a *continuity of growth* over many lifetimes. He will be shown his weaknesses and his strengths—all that he needs to build upon in order to free himself from the karmic debts he has collected on the earth, astral, and possibly other planes.

He will be given the teachings, the training, and the necessary preparation in order to help him develop what he needs in his next incarnation. This is not given immediately, however, for the soul can choose his own pace and need not be hurried through the planes in the afterlife. This is why it may take centuries in your time for the soul to know what is best for his development when he once again returns to the physical body. The teachings of his guides, and the soul's own reflection on his ultimate direction, enable him to decide upon the highest purpose for his next sojourn on earth.

Your people should learn how to give maximum assistance to the entity who is "dying." By praying that the entity will heighten his awareness and experience a quickening in his evolution, you are providing positive energies which are important to the crossing over. Grief and sorrow by the persons remaining on the earth plane may have the effect of holding back a departed entity. It is important to release him to his spirit guides and teachers, and hasten his journey by sending love and understanding.

There is no such thing as an "inopportune" death. All entities have chosen *when* they will leave the earth plane in a particular incarnation. It is for this reason that each of you should begin each day in preparation for death. Understanding the meaning of death will greatly enhance your living of life on a day by day basis. *All persons will "die."* It is the illusion of time which creates your misunderstanding.

If you lived each day as if it were your last one on earth, and as if it were everybody's last day, then your whole perspective of interaction with people would dramatically change. You would know that persons you met in hostility you would have to meet again in another realm. You would realize that any negativity in a relationship should be worked out immediately, not postponed.

You have perhaps heard the saying that you should never go to bed at night with hate in your heart. This is the guideline for working out all karma as soon as it is created. It is also one of the best techniques in preparing yourself for death.

HELPING OTHERS WHO ARE FACING DEATH

When persons are sick and know that they will soon be passing on, the most important way to help is to discuss with them the whole subject of death. Unfortunately, most people try to sweep death under a rug and hide it.

But a person's cross-over, or change in vibratory rate, should be something which is talked over, faced, and accepted among doctor, patient, family, and friends. In this way the final days

which you have together in this particular incarnation can be ones of great sharing and great
beauty.

If each soul could be taught a simple meditation technique at least ten days before death,
he would not fear it. He would find that during
the meditation he would be gently lifted out of
the body. He would then understand that he
is not dependent upon the body for life. By
going within through meditation the entity
would realize that he is not going to be experiencing *finality*, but rather a *progression*. He
is not "leaving" loved ones, only casting off
a physical body in order to go about his tasks
unhampered by physical matter.

Impending death should not put people in
uncomfortable positions, for this makes it very
hard on everyone involved. When people
approach death in fear, great amounts of energy
are drained from both family and patient. If
people would be open and honest, they could
help prepare a soul for his passing—which is
nothing more than *a birth into a new form*.
Souls must continue to move to planes or levels
where they can best function and accomplish
the greatest amount of growth.

From our point of view it is you who are dead
and not those crossing over. For in physical

matter the finer awarenesses and under-
standings are dulled. The life of awareness is
the life of the spirit.

▲

Death is no stranger to Betty. Through many
painful experiences she has learned to understand and accept death among her friends and
in her own family. It is her personal experience
which convinces her that "there is no death!"
As others catch from Betty this conviction
of hope and confidence, they also gain new perspectives. They are able to replace grief with
joy.

Chapter Five

EXPLORING
THE PSYCHIC REALM

Psychic phenomena, those unexplainable events which defy present scientific knowledge, are being widely studied today. Popularly lumped under the "ESP" banner, these phenomena include experiences such as telepathy, clairvoyance, clairaudience, precognition, and psychokinesis. Parapsychology is the emerging science which studies them.

Officially recognized in 1969 by the American Association for the Advancement of Science, parapsychology is a diverse field which numbers among its practitioners medical doctors, physicists, psychologists, biologists, chemists, electrical engineers, and psychics themselves. All are directing their efforts to try to understand how and why psychic phenomena do indeed occur.

Maybe you have a vivid dream about a specific future event—and it really happens (precognition). Or perhaps you have a feeling that a good friend is in trouble—and later find out that at that very moment he was in an automobile accident (telepathy). Or you are suddenly aware that a particular event is occurring miles away from you—you "see" it in your mind's eye simultaneously as it is happening (clairvoyance). Maybe you even find yourself capable of moving an object by thinking about it (psychokinesis). Such examples are typical of these unexplainable experiences people really have. In addition, some persons claim to see "entities" or "ghosts," others hear voices from no identifiable source, and still others report seeing pulsating energy fields within and around human beings and other life forms.

Traditional physics has no ready explanations. And the "scientific response" until quite recently has been to say that such things in fact don't happen, they are just coincidence, or just one's imagination.

Because of this attitude serious research has been slow in getting off the ground. It was less than 100 years ago that a group of scholars got together and founded the British Society for Psychical Research. Later William James was instrumental in forming a similar organization in the United States.

In higher education, scholars in some European and Eastern universities were seriously exploring the psychic realm by the turn of the century. Beginnings were later made in the United States at such schools as Harvard and Stanford (which were later discontinued), and in 1930 the parapsychology laboratory at Duke University was established.

Since that time, especially in the last decade, other universities in the United States and around the world have established parapsychological laboratories. A growing number are offering academic courses in the field. And many private institutions are now promoting psychic research.

Why is there such an interest today in understanding telepathy, precognition, psychokinesis, and the like? In addition to a natural human curiosity, those who are working at the forefront of this field see what could be earth-shattering implications. In government, in education, in medicine—in almost every area of daily living—knowing how to operate these phenomena at will could revolutionize our way of life. What would precognition and clairvoyance do to government secrecy, to warfare, to the educational system? How would telepathy affect the entire structure of modern communication systems?

The study of psychic phenomena appears to be prompted by an underlying desire to learn what the potentialities of man actually are.

In an effort to discover the laws which govern
these phenomena, we are realizing that our
concept of the universe—and our ideas about
its basic energy or stuff —may have to be
greatly expanded.

One way to discover more about these phenomena is to work with people—called psychics—
who frequently experience, and perhaps can
control, these events. But it is difficult to find
genuine psychics who are willing to work with
reputable researchers. And, until very recently,
it has been difficult to find reputable researchers
who approach the field with open-minded
objectivity.

Dr. William Tiller, professor and former
head of the department of Materials Science
at Stanford University, is an eminent physicist
who has been working with Betty. He recently
returned from a "psychic discoveries" trip to the
Soviet Union. He is himself working on experiments in acupuncture and related areas.

Dr. Tiller, one of the directors of the Academy
of Parapsychology and Medicine, approaches his
study from two perspectives. On the one hand,
he is the scientist—objective and analytical. On
the other hand, he is one who has practiced
meditation for the last seven years, and has
sought to experience some of the subtler realms
of being. The combination of the sensitive

scientist, Dr. Tiller, and the cooperative psychic, Betty Bethards, is unusual and promising.

This chapter introduces the reader to their dialogue on a variety of topics in the psychic phenomena spectrum. Of particular interest is the emphasis placed on the nature of time and space. For apparently a limited knowledge of these components is the largest single factor which prevents adequate understanding of man's psychic abilities, of his full potentialities.

Questions in this chapter are addressed either to Uvalla, Betty's primary guide (responding through her, of course), or to Dr. Tiller.

(It is of interest to note that the responses from Uvalla to the questions on space, time, and energy were given about one month before the responses by Dr. Tiller—who had no prior knowledge of Uvalla's comments.)

ONE OF THE PUZZLES IN PSYCHIC RESEARCH CONCERNS THE NATURE OF TIME—HOW SOME PEOPLE ARE ABLE TO "SEE" BOTH FUTURE AND PAST EVENTS. HOW WOULD YOU DESCRIBE TIME AS IT RELATES TO THE PSYCHIC REALM?

(Uvalla) Time as you know it matters only on your plane of existence. You accept the sequence of time in order to keep yourselves aligned to the days and the seasons, and to the stages you see in man's life process—from infancy to old age.

Time provides a point of reference. But it is
a schedule which earth dwellers get much
too involved in. What time really is, few men
understand. For all things have existed and all
things shall continue to exist throughout eternity.

In actuality, time is a vibratory rate. Time
is energy. As with all "things," one can attune
himself to the rate of vibration of time and
know it.

IS THIS HOW A PSYCHIC IS ABLE TO SEE THINGS
IN THE FUTURE OR IN THE PAST?

(Uvalla) Psychics for the most part are
tapping the astral realm, and there is no time on
that level. They may "see" either future or
past events. But picking up predictions is very
tricky. There has to be a heavy vibrational
rate around a thought form or event in order
for it to be pin-pointed. Very few have the
ability to interpret correctly the vibrational
rates on the astral plane. And if you had this
ability, you wouldn't want to spend that much
time on the astral.

Few psychics are developed to the point
where they can maintain the heightened vibration needed to draw from this realm continuously. Instead, they have flashes, or periods of
heightened sensitivity, during which they
perceive certain things.

A psychic may pick up facts about another person because he is attuning to the vibrations of that person. The entity's force field, or energy field, carries a life plan within it. Yet again, it is often difficult to determine whether the event is a past, present, or future occurrence in the person's incarnation.

APPARENTLY, THEN, YOU SEE TIME AS A FINITE ENERGY LEVEL. HOW ABOUT SPACE?

(Uvalla) Space, like time, is an energy. The clairvoyant who is able to see what is happening in another part of the world at the exact moment it is occurring is attuning to the "space vibration." Or, if the person is able to see entities around him who are out of the body, he has raised his rate of vibration to their frequency. You tend to think in terms of objects and people when you talk of attuning to vibrations. Yet the gases which make up the air you breathe have vibratory rates. It is difficult to imagine attuning yourself to the same vibration as "air"—much less to another *dimension* called *space*.

TRADITIONAL SCIENCE, OF COURSE, HAS QUESTIONED THE REALITY OF BOTH CLAIRVOYANCE AND PRECOGNITION—NOT TO MENTION SOME OF THE OTHER PHENOMENA.

(Uvalla) Yes, because the majority of scientists have not understood space and time as energies. There are persons now who do understand this, but their research, for the most part, has not been revealed.

ARE EXPERIMENTS ON THE NATURE OF TIME BEING CONDUCTED IN THE SOVIET UNION?

(Dr. Tiller) Yes, there are experiments going on at a university in Leningrad. The man conducting these has great ability and considerable reputation. He looks at time as an energy, and is certainly far away from the general thinking of his colleagues.

WHAT DO YOU PERSONALLY THINK ABOUT THE CONCEPTS OF TIME AND SPACE?

(Dr. Tiller) My own feeling is that we will eventually learn that space and time are properties of waves at the mind and spirit level, the same way as mass and charge are properties of waves at the electro-magnetic level. What this would mean, then, is that time and space are indeed forms of energy. And that by the use of the mind, one can "deform" space and time and thus control them.

There is much information that seems to be pointing out to us that there are dimensions of the universe we know little about, but that are somehow synchronized with our own. Some of these dimensions have very different space-time coordinates than our familiar Einsteinian frame, and some of them seem to be without the limitations of space or time.

WOULD YOU ELABORATE ON THESE OTHER DIMENSIONS OF THE UNIVERSE?

(Dr. Tiller) The Russians refer to the "bio-plasmic realm." Others speak of the "etheric plane." My feeling is that there are several interpenetrating universes, and within this synchronized regime there are material substances within substances within substances—and so on. So this may mean that we have bodies—energy bodies—which would be unobstructed, without the restraints of time and space.

These are different energies than we know anything about, and they obey different laws. We know basically about one kind of stuff, and at this time evidence is suggestive of perhaps seven different kinds of stuff. There is only enough information to suggest that we start looking very seriously for these new energies.

HOW WOULD YOU EXPLAIN MAN'S RELATION TO TIME AND SPACE, AND HIS ABILITY TO EXTEND BEYOND THESE?

(Uvalla) Mankind allows both time and space to rule his life. He does not realize he is free from these dimensions. Once he gains a full understanding of these he will not be limited.

People must learn that although they perceive themselves to be in physical bodies, made up of denser matter, they are not prisoners in these bodies. The finer energies within them, their "spirits," are free to go into limitless eternity seeking all knowledge and learning all things. This limitless freedom exists not only for teachers and masters, but for each individual soul.

WHY CAN'T MEN PERCEIVE THESE FINER ENERGIES NOW?

(Uvalla) Some do. But men receive this understanding only as they are able to use it, and apply it directly to their "24 hour a day" lives. A man will never be given more of the teachings than he himself can grasp within his own framework of understanding.

These apparent limitations of time and space prohibit man from abusing the power which is within him. As you learn to live and experience the higher teachings, you may safely receive more. Your spiritual development is essential to using this power wisely. For if you knew the secret to all energies—and everything is energy—you would be able to control your universe.

THIS KNOWLEDGE IS OPEN TO ALL PERSONS?

(Uvalla) That's correct. Through meditation one can learn to understand and go beyond these limited realms. By going within, knowing yourself, and understanding your potentialities—this is the way to be freed for living in the now of eternity.

IT SEEMS WE ARE BEGINNING TO DISCOVER MORE ABOUT SOME OF THE INNER ENERGY SYSTEMS OF MAN THROUGH ACUPUNCTURE. WHAT IS THE PRESENT STATUS OF ACUPUNCTURE?

(Dr. Tiller) It shouldn't work according to American medicine. But it is found to be effective according to British, European and Eastern medicine—it works there and has been operating effectively for a long time.

I was in London about a year ago and had acupuncture done. I was suffering from a serious indigestion problem. I went to a doctor, and she demonstrated how acupuncture works. She felt the various pulses on the wrist, then said I had problems with the gall bladder and liver meridians. She then used an instrument which measured indications at various acupuncture points on the body to determine which of these particular circuits were affected. Then she knew where to put the needles, or which points of the body to stimulate. The treatment was completely successful.

WHAT WAS THIS INSTRUMENT
SHE WAS USING?

(Dr. Tiller) The instrument measures the
resistance of the skin. We have built one and
I am now studying it at Stanford. You will
find that the skin resistance is on the order of
a couple of million ohms generally. But if you
touch an acupuncture point with this instrument you find that the resistance drops to
something like 100,000 ohms. The device is
designed to give you a signal (a light or a
sound) when you've touched a localized point
of low resistance.

As we locate these various points we see that
they correspond to those on the ancient Chinese
charts. So the map is already available. With
our present instruments we sometimes identify
additional points as well.

WHAT IS THE PURPOSE OF THE NEEDLES?
HOW DO THEY MAKE ACUPUNCTURE WORK?

(Dr. Tiller) You can use needles, a chemical
stimulus, massage, an electrical impulse, a beam
of laser light, or the injection of energy from a
psychic. My own postulation of what's going
on is that perhaps there is another circulatory
system of the body we know nothing about. It
might be on a par with the blood, lymph, and
nervous systems.

I postulate that anyway, because it brings the whole process out in the open—rather than saying the individual is hypnotized, or it "has something to do with the nerves." And we will find out eventually if it is a fluidic circuit as suggested by the ancient Chinese.

Generally, in the fluid circuits of the body, there are little particles called colloids that flow down the tubules. They are very important energy aspects of the body. Now if the body is in balance, if it is healthy, the little particles will flow regularly and there is no problem because they remain dispersed.

However, if the body is out of balance, then you get a type of coagulation phenomena. We're familiar with this in heart conditions—blood clots, and so on. In any case, these particles agglomerate, and they form a raft that is moving down one of these tubules. We might think of the acupuncture points as stations at which there is an eddy in the stream. So the raft may get hung up, and the fluid piles up behind this blockage, just as it does in a normal stream. Then it takes a greater amount of energy to move the fluid through the stream, so you can develop an imbalance between that limb of the circuit and some other limb of the circuit. That imbalance starts to cause ill health. It diverts energy from certain parts of the body to others and creates environmental conditions in which bacteria can grow. These various disharmonies can manifest in the forms we see as disease.

These are speculated reasons why acupuncture works. But at the moment we don't know. We haven't done a lot of serious studies yet to trace this down.

BUT ACUPUNCTURE INVOLVES A BALANCING EFFECT ON THE BODY?

(Dr. Tiller) Yes, apparently so. The Russians have found that by measuring the same acupuncture point on both right and left sides of the body they get a certain resistance. If they then turn the electrodes around and measure in the reverse direction, there is the same resistance—if the individual is healthy. But if the individual is unhealthy in respect to that gland or area, there is a difference in the resistance. The degree of difference is proportional to the degree of disease.

Some Russian scientists did an experiment in which they used a healer to project energy to a sick person whose circuits were unbalanced. They measured some six or seven points on the patient and on the healer before the experiment. The patient showed an imbalance, the healer did not.

Then after the projection of healing they measured the ill person again, and his differential resistance had decreased—which meant

he was getting healthier. The healer's resistance
had increased. He seemed to have partially
unbalanced his own circuits in order to help
balance the patient.

YOU HAVE TRIED EXPERIMENTS OF YOUR OWN?

(Dr. Tiller) Yes, we thought we'd do a
similar experiment. I had an acupuncture
device, and my wife had an abdominal problem.
And Betty Bethards was a local healer. The
points for my wife's abdomen happened to be
on the side of the knees. So I measured from
left to right, and from right to left, and got
a difference in resistance of about twenty per
cent. I measured Betty and there was no
difference.

Betty projected healing into the acupuncture
points at the knees, and the resistance changed
on both of them. But the difference was still
there. I said, "Okay, just put it in the one knee."
And she did, but the difference increased
because I picked the wrong knee!

Uvalla, communicating through Betty, said
it wasn't necessary to put this kind of energy
into the knees, but to put it into the back of the
neck. He explained that the body has its own
intelligence in terms of knowing where best to
use this kind of energy. Betty then projected
energy into the back of the neck, and I measured
the resistances—they had changed. I measured

them daily for about a week and a half. The resistance at these places had doubled in magnitude, which meant the health condition had gone up. Then, there was no longer any differential resistance—and the abdominal condition was gone.

BESIDES TRYING TO LEARN MORE ABOUT THE ENERGY SYSTEMS AND MERIDIANS WITHIN THE BODY, WORK HAS ALSO BEEN DONE IN CONNECTION WITH THE HUMAN ENERGY FIELD, OR "AURA." DID YOU SEE SOME OF THIS WORK IN RUSSIA?

(Dr. Tiller) In Russia, and now in this country, there have been experiments with what is called Kirlian photography. It is a high voltage photography for detecting energy leaving the skin. The camera responds to electromagnetic energy, although I think there is much more coming out of the skin than just the electromagnetic. Basically what is thought to happen is that electrons are sucked out of the skin and they move across the air gap. They accelerate, hit molecules, and give off bursts of light. That's what exposes the film.

Under a microscope we can observe flares of energy coming out of the body at acupuncture points. Depending on whether a person is tired, emotionally or mentally excited, the color and energy intensity from these flare points changes. When a healer's hands were photographed as he was projecting healing energy, spots of light appeared from many acupuncture points.

Initially the Russians thought they were seeing what clairvoyants have called the aura, but now they aren't sure exactly what is being recorded. They took a leaf and cut part of it away. When they photographed the remaining part, there was an energy pattern of the *whole* leaf. They suggested this might be related to the lost limb effect—when a person loses an arm or leg and still has sensation in the phantom limb.

Two things come to mind. First of all, the main energy they see is cold electron emission coming out of acupuncture points from the leaf. But secondly, this phenomenon suggests that at some deeper level of substance there is a radiation from coherent energy sources which would give rise to a pattern of energy like a hologram. This hologram might provide the force field which allows the organization of matter at a physical level. This matter would take on, or follow, the pattern given from this other level.

Now that's very consistent with our idea of interpenetrating universes.

AND THIS WOULD HAVE SIGNIFICANT IMPLICATIONS IN MEDICINE?

(Dr. Tiller) If this bears out with future

experiments, then it implies that if an individual loses a leg the primary energy pattern of the leg will still be there. If we know how to work with this pattern, and feed it cellular material in the right way, then we may indeed be able to grow a new leg—just like a salamander can.

Some experiments have been done in which the muscle of a rat was removed, ground up, and then fed back into the open cavity from which the muscle was originally taken. After a few weeks the experimenters found that, in fact, the muscle became reorganized in the appropriate pattern.

So the possibility of working with cellular substances and applying them to organizing energy patterns indeed exists.

HOW WOULD YOU DESCRIBE THIS ENERGY
FIELD, OR AURA?

(Uvalla) The aura is made up of interpenetrating energy fields, and is beyond the electromagnetic range. It consists of what we call bio-energy, the life energy, which you have virtually no concept of at this time.

You'll find that the frequency is as fast as thought—if you can but imagine this—and this is why it has not been photographed with any degree of success. For thought is faster than the speed of light.

UNDERSTANDING THE POWER OF THOUGHT
WOULD HELP US UNDERSTAND HOW
PSYCHOKINESIS OPERATES.

(Uvalla) The psychokinetic experiments going on today are hardly scratching the surface. By way of a comparison, the pyramids were built by this thought process. Rocks were cut out, lifted up, and placed into position by concentrated thought energy from a group in a circle.

WHAT CAN WE HOPE TO LEARN THROUGH THE
STUDY OF PYRAMIDS IN EGYPT?

(Uvalla) The pyramids were built in order to preserve the knowledge of the Atlanteans, their secrets for understanding the powerful energies of the universe. Potentially these could destroy the human race. And man is not yet ready spiritually again to discover these secrets.

The pyramids are situated on powerful vibratory fields of the earth plane. There is a vibrant magnetism going up from the earth through the center of the pyramid, and this combined with the forces from the sun and planetary influences gives you a power far stronger than you can imagine. Atlantis was also built on such a field.

BACK TO PSYCHOKINESIS AS SUCH. HAVE YOU
SEEN SOME EXPERIMENTS?

(Dr. Tiller) In Russia I have seen experiments in psychokinesis. They were impressive.
The most impressive example was when I was
in a restaurant in Leningrad. Nelya Kulagina
came into the restaurant and sat down next
to me at my table. There were a number of us
there to investigate the Russian work. She took
off her wedding ring and placed it on the table
about three or four feet from her. She sat back
with her hands clasped and just looked at it.
She twisted her head a little bit, and the ring
started to move across the table.

Now I am a physicist, brought up on Newtonian physics and Einstein type physics. I found
myself having to think that maybe there are
some other forces and aspects of physics operative in the universe that we don't know anything
about.

I saw another individual who was just
learning to move objects. She was able to roll
an object. This is an easier task, for it involves
only the resistance of rolling friction, whereas
the other involves moving a whole mass and
overcoming static friction.

WHAT DO YOU THINK THE PRINCIPLE OF
PSYCHOKINESIS MIGHT BE?

(Dr. Tiller) I don't think any of us understands it. From my observations I think the

Russians have found that there is an energy manifestation in the vicinity of the object. They find that this energy field pulsates. The respiration rate, the alpha waves, and the heart rhythm of the sender all come into synchronization. And they find that when they move the energy detector from the object towards the sender, they reach a domain where they no longer pick up the energy, almost as if the energy utilizes some other pathway and appears in the vicinity of the object. Now in terms of our conventional physics that's not the way things would operate. I don't think we've even begun to understand what's really happening.

WHILE YOU WERE IN RUSSIA, WHAT ELSE DID YOU SEE THAT IMPRESSED YOU?

(Dr. Tiller) The telepathy work is impressive. The Russians have done many experiments, some with rabbits. In one such experiment they hooked a mother rabbit up to an encephalograph, then took her babies down under the ocean in a submarine. They killed them, one by one. Every time one was killed a change in the brain pattern of the mother was recorded. This showed that there was a linkage between the children and the mother, and that the transmission of awareness was not by electromagnetic energy.

DO YOU THINK THAT TELEPATHY IS FAIRLY
COMMON AMONG HUMANS?

(Dr. Tiller) I suspect that there is much more
communication of a non-physical nature among
people than we realize. A person can be thought
of as a radio station operating on a particular
band of frequencies and at a particular power
level. But the radiation is just not in the electro-
magnetic spectrum as far as I'm concerned.
We've yet to prove that, although there have
been experiments where people were put in
Faraday cages—which should rule out the
electro-magnetic theory.

DO YOU RELATE TELEPATHY TO THE ENERGY
CENTERS, OR CHAKRAS, OF THE BODY?

(Dr. Tiller) Yes, as we get into this we need
to consider the Eastern literature and the
chakras. The endocrine glands function at a
physical level, and I think the chakras are at
the next finer level of substance. And these
act much like a transducer—they receive, trans-
duct, and then broadcast energy. If you are a
high power station you can walk into a room
and people will feel it.

WHAT ELSE IS GOING ON IN THE
SOVIET UNION THAT YOU FOUND
PARTICULARLY INTERESTING?

(Dr. Tiller) Perhaps the work on what is
called "artificial reincarnation." This is a form

of dynamic hypnosis in which you suggest to people that they are principal figures from the past—and they take on the characteristics of those figures. You can take an individual who plays the piano only adequately, who is interested and does a bit of training. Under this type of hypnosis you can suggest that he is a famous concert pianist. The transformation one sees in his ability is really great—professionals themselves say he is playing like a professional.

When you take the individual out of this state of consciousness, he has this increased ability to some degree, but it fades after about five days. If you continue to have the individual practice during this five day period, and alter his state of consciousness back and forth, between the normal and the hypnotized state, then you can transfer some of this ability to his normal consciousness. You can keep taking a person into this hypnotic state, and then out, and over a period of about a year his ability to perform with these talents may increase ten to one hundred fold.

I saw the work of a young girl who had been a physics student, and not particularly interested in art. By using this technique, suggesting that she was a famous artist, she was drawing at the level of commercial artists at the end of a year. In fact, she was thinking of changing her profession.

THIS SAYS QUITE A LOT ABOUT THE
POWER OF THOUGHT.

(Dr. Tiller) Yes, in essence we could all be
great with respect to a particular talent. Now
I think we can do this with ourselves just by
self-suggestion. It's done with our own mind!
We can tap that level of consciousness that
contains the ability, and make it consciously
ours.

AFTER HAVING BEEN TO RUSSIA, WOULD YOU
SAY THAT THEIR RESEARCH IS GENERALLY
AHEAD OF THAT IN OTHER COUNTRIES?

(Dr. Tiller) First of all, it's very hard to
say how far ahead of us they are. Much of it
is underground. But that which we've seen is
fantastic.

I know that they have been working on it
very strongly since about 1960, after Stalin's
death. And, of course, they did a lot of good
work back in the thirties. Now it's government
sponsored.

I think we saw just a little bit of the iceberg.
So I can't really make any comparisons.

WHAT SPECIFIC AREA DO YOU THINK
PSYCHICAL RESEARCH SHOULD PURSUE NOW?

(Uvalla) The importance of psychical research at this particular time lies in bringing

science and religion together. Once science accepts *survival* of the soul, a new harmony will emerge. A new understanding of the universal laws and how matter and energy are combined to work together will result.

But right now some researchers have abandoned experiments which try to prove survival beyond physical death because of the difficulty in establishing such proof.

(Uvalla) This is very true. Right now researchers are using mediums who are going to the astral level and contacting entities. Much of the information is unreliable. This is not where you are going to find your proof of survival. Your proof must come from an understanding of the energy field which is within you, from finding out that you are not limited to this body. By being able to establish proof of this energy field, you will know it is *that* which goes on.

Why do you think there is such a keen interest in psychic phenomena today?

(Uvalla) You are moving into a period where the expansion of awareness is being accelerated for many people, and they are experiencing psychic happenings. Unfortunately, if they have not been meditating, they will not know how to control this energy — or they will control, but misuse it. The next two year period is a critical one. The veil between physical and etheric worlds is thinning, and it is very important that people learn how to use wisely these new sensitivities.

HOW DO YOU AS A SCIENTIST ACCOUNT FOR THE GROWING INTEREST IN PSYCHIC PHENOMENA TODAY?

(Dr. Tiller) I think it's worth saying that at this point in time it appears that there is an increase in this kind of energy in the universe. Therefore, many people are picking up this energy. It's moving in their organism and they don't understand it. They have feelings they don't understand and so they are frightened. And they try to block it. But trying to block this energy is like having a cat loose inside of you. This energy is going to build up in certain places and then discharge through the body. It will probably be through some aspect of the nervous system, and could "burn off" some of the insulation, so to speak.

If one keeps going on in this way, he begins to have uncontrolled fear. The body may begin to do things the individual didn't intend for it to do, and one moves toward a type of schizophrenia. I think many people today are suffering from this. In fact, their own weaknesses start being accentuated. It is mainly because there is an energy in the system that people don't know how to work with or how to use.

HOW CAN THEY LEARN TO USE THIS ENERGY?

(Dr. Tiller) Meditation makes you increasingly more coherent in terms of passage of energy through your body. You can actually function with much greater energy in both your day-to-day business and family life and in the "extra" sensory aspects of your life.

But one can have a sense of imbalance with meditation as well. If an individual starts meditation and does it virtually all day long, then his life becomes very unbalanced and he no longer works in the "real" world.

Meditation can be used in a passive sense to merely escape from the turmoil and stresses of the physical world we live in (and many use it this way). Or, it can be used in a dynamic sense to enhance perception, regenerate vitality, and focus attention on coherent courses of action to resolve the seeming dilemmas of the physical world around us; that is, it makes us more capable of effective action.

Generally, meditation is beneficial to one when he oscillates between the state of consciousness associated with the external world and his work there—because that's where he tests his responses—and then oscillates back into this altered state of consciousness in meditation. It is here that you will sense the wide panorama of your inner life, in my judgment, and integrate or bring continuity to the total self.

SO PRACTICING MEDITATION HELPS ONE UNDERSTAND PSYCHIC ENERGY. HOW IS THE PSYCHIC ACTUALLY RELATED TO "SPIRITUAL" MAN?

(Uvalla) Psychic ability really has nothing to do with spirituality. Many people have psychic sensitivity but are spiritually unaware.

Spirituality can grow from this psychic ability—if the person comes to realize that the universe offers much more than he had ever imagined.

The psychic energy is certainly a higher frequency than the average man is able to use. But the spiritual energy, or realm, is a qualitatively different dimension.

MYSTICS AS WELL AS PSYCHICS CLAIM TO EXPERIENCE A REALM BEYOND TIME. HOW WOULD YOU DESCRIBE A MYSTIC, AND WHAT IS HE EXPERIENCING?

(Uvalla) A mystic is an entity who looks strictly to the Universal Intelligence, to God, for his answers. The mystic may move freely within the seven planes. This is why he will have the highest visions, and experience the most profound truths. He is beyond any enchantment with phenomena.

This state of awareness comes through many incarnations of working in the occult (which is a lower form), in healing, and in channeling. Mysticism is the elite of gifts or achievements. The true mystical experience is the closest thing to Nirvana.

CAN YOU DESCRIBE NIRVANA?

(Uvalla) It defies description. Simply, it is a peace, an attunement to all forces. You may move freely throughout the planes of the universe. You have the ability to know the beauty within each soul, no matter what plane of life it is on.

WOULD YOU SAY THAT NIRVANA CORRESPONDS TO HAVING ALL THE CHAKRAS OPEN AND CONTROLLED?

(Uvalla) No. Many people have their chakras open, or have the crown chakra open, but still do not know what Nirvana is. It is a qualitatively different state of energy attunement.

Many are highly illumined, but have not yet experienced this. Many masters today claim to have done so, but there are, in fact, only a handful on the earth plane who have experienced it.

EARLIER YOU MENTIONED THAT MAN,
POTENTIALLY, IS ABLE TO CONTROL TIME. AND
IT IS SAID THAT "SPIRITUAL" PEOPLE OFTEN
APPEAR AGELESS.

(Uvalla) People who are meditating slow down the aging process. They often retain a youthful look, due to the high vibrations within them. For meditation actually changes every cell in the body.

Sorrow, misery and unhappiness are part of what causes man to age. If he were at peace and harmony within himself, he would not age nearly so quickly.

HOW DO YOU THINK MEDITATION MIGHT BE
RELATED TO THE TIME PROCESS, OR TO HEALTH?

(Dr. Tiller) I feel that meditation does, indeed, change the cells in one's body, for it is a harmonizing process. It literally can have a rejuvenating effect.

The Russians have shown, for example, that if you project negative thoughts to an individual you can decrease the white cell count of the body. By sending positive thoughts you can increase the white cell count—hence the person would tend to have immmunity to disease.

Thought, meditation, can indeed affect the bodily processes.

IT WOULD SEEM, THEN, THAT WE HAVE ONLY BEGUN TO REALIZE WHAT SOME OF THE VAST POTENTIALITIES OF MAN MIGHT BE. IN CLOSING, DO YOU HAVE ANY COUNSEL AS TO THE MOST EFFECTIVE WAY TO CONTINUE EXPLORATION OF THE PSYCHIC—AND OTHER—REALMS?

(Uvalla) As you continue to explore the psychic dimension — and beyond — you will discover that understanding must be integrally related to the evolution of your own consciousness.

Meditation is the process which regulates and speeds up this evolution, for it attunes you to the finer energies of the universe. When you understand the powerful forces within, you will know the reality behind all phenomena, all things.

Chapter Six

PROBLEMS
AND PROMISE
OF OUR AGE

Are we living in a time of special importance
as compared with other periods of human
history? According to some mystics and seers,
as well as to students of astrology, we are
presently entering a new era often labeled the
"Age of Aquarius."

The primary characteristic of this age is
supposed to be accelerated spiritual evolution.
As a world community we clearly face grave
problems. Is the human spirit also developing
new resources for dealing with these dilemmas?

Betty's guides speak of the significance of
this period from the context of karmic ties with
earlier civilizations. Particularly important for
the United States is its karmic tie with
Atlantis—the much discussed lost continent.

Atlantis is very real to Betty's teachers. They explain it was a highly advanced technological society, predating ancient Egypt, and located off the southeastern coast of the United States. The remaining fringes of this continent are said to be the Bahamas and other islands in the same region. Knowledge of the ancient civilization and many of its secrets, they suggest, are still to be found in the pyramids of Egypt, and possibly also in South America.

The Atlanteans were highly developed intellectually, yet they adopted inhumane laws and customs. They became materialistic, negative, and hostile in their relations with one another. Their negative thought vibrations caused disruptive forces in the earth—and their entire continent sank!

Many of the Atlanteans, reportedly, are now back. They have incarnated in the United States for the most part, because the technological advancements (though not as great), and the general period of war and hostility, approximate the climate of the ill-fated Atlantis. We are assured that we now have another chance to pull things together. But if we don't, the negative, destructive thought vibrations we are perpetuating through war, prejudice, and lack of caring about others will again result in wide-scale destruction.

Years ago the psychic Edgar Cayce predicted great land mass changes. These would occur, he said, not only on the east and west coasts of our country, but in other places around the world. This, he pointed out, could be prevented, but man would have to change his orientation toward his fellows, toward his total environment.

In an age when ecology is being widely discussed, we may need to expand our concept of interdependent relationships. Perhaps man's energy forces—mental, physical, emotional and spiritual—interpenetrate and affect the vibrations of his total world. A balanced world, an ecologically sound environment, may depend on the harmonizing of these energies. In the following interview Betty's guides consider many of these issues.

WHAT IS THE IMPORTANCE OF THE AGE
IN WHICH WE NOW LIVE?

The point in time you are living in is particularly important for the future direction of mankind. Your country and your world must join hands in brotherhood or they will destroy themselves within (what you would call) the next several decades.

This is a time of great testing, but also a time of breakthrough. As we have said, the "veil" between physical and etheric worlds is becoming much thinner. And people who have always scoffed at psychic phenomena or spirituality will suddenly awaken to the reality of these realms once again.

The vibrations of the earth—from our perspective—are becoming worn and tired. This is due to all the disharmony and negativity in the world—the wars, the hatred, the violence. Such vibrations result in physical disasters. These vibrations must be changed, and the time for starting this is now. Otherwise, you will not survive much beyond the turn of the century.

There is a great shadow hanging over the earth today—one of destruction, one of sickness, one of great sorrow. There is a loss of hope, a loss of the sense of unity, a loss of love. If mankind is to survive the guilt, the fears, the bitterness, and the hatred he has brought upon himself, he must return to the God within him. Only in this way will he know all men are brothers.

You can return to the God within through the tools which you were given individually when you incarnated on the earth plane. For *within* you lie all the things you will ever need to survive in your lifetime. You need nothing other than that which you already have.

THEN THIS AGE DOES HAVE A UNIQUE
IMPORTANCE?

Yes, the "Age of Aquarius" is a time when the
forces around the earth are changing into a
spiritual vibration. The way to participate
in this change—to grow with this change—is to
learn from the "university within." Otherwise,
the coarse vibrations which result from men not
attuning to the emerging finer energies will
cause their own destruction—at least for this
age. And such persons will have to wait, perhaps
through eons of your time, before they again
will be able to work out karmic debts.

THE MAIN IMPORTANCE IS ON THE KARMIC
LEVEL?

Yes. Man must work out his karma in the
plane of space and time and on your planet.
He cannot escape the laws of sowing and
reaping.

You as a people, and as individuals, are
working out karmic ties. Your conditions on the
earth plane are similar to the conditions or
vibrations during the Atlantean period. At the
time of Atlantis, the people chose not to unite
in harmony. They continued on their own paths,
in selfishness and deceit. They sought mainly
material comforts and pleasures. They were
destroyed, so to speak, not by God, but by

themselves. The vibrations they generated into the atmosphere and into the center of the earth literally boomeranged—and they reaped what they had sown.

Now, again, you are sitting on a time bomb. The vibrations going down to the center of the earth are at a boiling point, a crucial point. If they explode, continents will go down, others will rise—and wide scale destruction will prevail.

WHAT WOULD HAPPEN THEN?

You would have to start all over again. You would work your way back through time and space, where the vibrations are again the same as you would have left them. You would have to wait until conditions on your plane were again identical, and then you would reincarnate and do the job which you have not done this time. This is why most of the Atlanteans are back now. You must eventually work out that karma. If you are lax now, and go your own way, you will return.

WHAT IS YOUR TASK IN THIS?

We are trying to prevent the destruction of mankind and the start of the entire process over again. We are helping to accelerate the changing of the earth's vibrations into a spiritual vibration. It is our job from this side, and your job on the earth plane, to unite mankind in love.

We feel your hurts and sufferings, and we see the sorrow in mankind. We are trying to get you to unite your efforts, so that all can move into a happier, higher vibration together.

IS THERE A PARTICULAR SIGNIFICANCE FOR THE YEAR 2000 A.D.?

By 2002 you are going to know beyond a doubt which way mankind is going. If he continues abusing the earth, abusing his brothers, ignoring the total ecology of the earth vibration, then he cannot survive much beyond 2024.

WHAT IS THE VALUE OF ASTROLOGY IN UNDERSTANDING OUR PRESENT SITUATION?

For the most part present day astrology serves as a kindergartner's tool. Astrology was a great science in the past. But most men do not have access to that knowledge. You'll find that many of the secrets are going to be learned from Egypt.

YOU MENTIONED THAT PEOPLE ARE BECOMING MORE SENSITIVE TO PSYCHIC ABILITY. DO YOU FEEL THERE WILL BE A GREAT INCREASE IN THE USE—OR MISUSE—OF THIS ABILITY?

As people become more keenly aware of the changing vibrations around them, their psychic ability will become much greater. Psychic energy has been used by persons who knew how to direct it for thousands of years. It has been used both for good and destructive purposes. It is already being used for destructive purposes in your world—much more than you realize. This energy in and of itself is a power—neither good nor bad. It is up to the user to determine its purposes.

These next several years will be severe ones for people who are developing this power rapidly, and don't know how to use it or control it. Karmically it is potent.

This is why it is so important to attune yourself to spiritual growth, to surround yourself in the white light of protection. Psychic knowledge must be used for peace, for love, for working together.

IS THE GROWING INTEREST IN EASTERN PHILOSOPHY AN INDICATION OF THIS EXPANDED AWARENESS?

It is time for Western people to be exposed to Eastern beliefs—and vice-versa—in order for mankind to unite. He must have a blending of the best from both Eastern and Western traditions. One's philosophy cannot be Eastern, it cannot be Western. You must take the essence of the concepts, the ideals, from both and bring them together. It is important that you have universal views. This is the key to understanding religions—to know about the underlying principles which unify men, not separate them.

Each person should be able to take what is right for himself from every faith, from every philosophy. Each should be given the free will to take that which he is suited for at this particular time in his evolution.

No one should force his way upon anyone else. For this would only result in another form of the ritualistic, dogmatic society you should be trying to get away from.

WHAT IS THE VALUE OF THE SCRIPTURES OF VARIOUS WORLD RELIGIONS, AS THEY SPEAK TO THE PROBLEMS OF OUR AGE?

The translations you read of any scriptures represent an individual's or several individuals' viewpoint. And you must not be bound by the period in which the scriptures may have been written. Take into consideration the time and culture of the writer. Often the writer was emphasizing dogma, or fear, to hold power over the people. The majority of the teachings are very right, however. Yet you must have ears to hear, and eyes to see.

Whether the words are found in the Bible, in the Koran, in the Bhagavad Gita—or any other sacred writings—all universal truth is the same. It is simply that God is love—the power, the energy, the vibration of love; and that you must do unto others as you would have them do unto you—love your brother (and all men are your brothers) as yourself. These are the two things which would create total peace and harmony.

Few people hear this. And yet it is in almost every language, in every country, taught by every master who has ever been a channel of God.

DO YOU THINK INTEREST IN YOGA HAS MUSHROOMED IN THE WEST BECAUSE OF THIS NEED FOR ATTUNEMENT TO THE FINER ENERGIES?

Yoga is an excellent discipline. It prepares the mental, the physical, and the spiritual. Yoga is one of the many ways whereby people are trying to discover the true meaning of self. Interest in yoga—in its many forms—is part of man's effort to gain a universal perspective.

HOW DO YOU SEE THE ORGANIZED CHURCH FITTING INTO THE EMERGING PERIOD?

The churches are undergoing a tremendous transitional period at this time. The Catholic Church in particular is going to have some of its greatest changes in the years immediately ahead.

There is a possibility that the organized church as such will fall. What people must learn is that there is one denomination, one God, for us all. It matters not which particular master or teacher a person may be drawn to. Remember, Jesus and other masters have said, "Not me, but my Father."

It is this teaching which must be understood if universal order is to come and mankind is to live in peace. Any time there is more than one church in power, or there are various dogmatic "religious" beliefs, there will be wars (such as you've seen in Ireland), there will be prejudice, and a pulling apart.

God is a united One who is within all people. If man could learn to worship in the temple he carries within him, then there would be no prejudice, no racial, political or religious wars. And this must come if you are to survive.

The churches have badly misinterpreted the teachings in the past. The many "dissections" of truth have resulted in a dissected human race—you are not a whole people. This surgery of the spirit has resulted in the monstrosity of hatred. Mankind *should have grown* in the unifying spirit of love.

BECAUSE OF THE COMPLEXITY OF THE AGE,
MANY PEOPLE SEEM TO BE CAUGHT UP IN
DESPAIR. HOW ARE WE TO DEAL WITH THIS?

There is a sense of hopelessness today, which
comes from man's lack of understanding of the
suffering he sees around him. Man finds the
world in confusion, and senses his inability to
respond and relate to things he finds offensive.

The key here is for souls to understand that
they can begin to relate hopefully and meaning-
fully to the world by loving, caring for, and
helping others. Too many people feel that they
by themselves can do nothing. But each of you is
an example, a channel, an instrument of God.
The more light or good you give out, the more
you dispel the hopelessness, meaninglessness, and
negativity around you. Once you realize that the
God within can and will use your channel—your
life—you will literally be able to change history.

For each of you casts a light—it can spread
over a mere speck of dust, or clear across the
world.

EARLIER YOU REFERRED TO ECOLOGY. WOULD
YOU COMMENT FURTHER HERE?

The current problem of pollution represents
part of the struggle of this particular age. Man
has abused the earth ever since he's been on it.

Because of the larger population now you are beginning to see the fruits of such misuse. People will have to become aware that they are destroying the very things they need for survival.

Uncontrolled population growth, limited food production, contaminated water supply, smog-ridden cities—lack of awareness has created problems in these and many other areas. Generally man has adopted the attitude, "Live for today and to hell (literally) with tomorrow."

But mind pollution is the originator of the outer manifestations. The ideas you saturate yourself with appear in outward form. Man's fanatical beliefs, his ignorance, his selfishness— all have created a pollution within himself. This must be cleared up first if he is to harmonize the forces of the earth.

WE ARE ENTERING A PERIOD WHICH IS MARKED BY WHAT SOME PEOPLE CALL "THE NEW MORALITY." HOW ARE OUR RELATIONSHIPS WITH OTHERS, OUR SEXUAL BEHAVIOR, AFFECTED BY THE AGE WE ARE PRESENTLY IN?

As man endeavors to get in touch with the deeper levels of being, he comes into contact with the powerful *life force*. This has been called the Kundalini power, or spirit energy, of man. This power is latent within all men, and is one

of the keys to spiritual evolution. It is the force
which makes all things possible to you.

This power expresses itself through the seven
primary chakras or energy centers in the body.
As it unfolds, man experiences certain sensations. Many people at present feel a manifestation of this energy through their second
chakra, which is experienced as the sexual
energy. This is only one expression of this
force—there are much higher levels. Understanding this force, and how it causes you to
interact with others, is important to understanding the divergent relationships in this
age—in your life.

This life force is what brought you into being
and it is what brings you back to the oneness
with God. It is a "creative" energy you must
learn to work with, adapt and adjust for your
own best growth in this incarnation. It draws
you to other people—it helps you realize that
the *real* in relationships is spirit, is energy—
it is something that one can *experience*, not
physically see.

What you term "morality," however, is a
product of man's laws. The laws you will be
judged by at the end of your present incarnation
have nothing to do with how many people you've
slept with. The morality which we live under
on our plane is universal law, and is very just.

You must love your fellows as you love yourself.
If there is hurt involved in any relationship—
whether through criticism, gossip, selfish desires,
rape, or cruelty of any kind—then there is a
karmic tie.

When you leave the earth plane, you will be
judged solely on whether you developed your
potential gifts, those which you carried to the
earth plane with you. Have you helped your
fellowman along life's path? Or ignored him
for your own selfish purposes?

Laws structuring human relationships were
laid down in ancient times in order to control
what was a vast immoral age. But the freedom
in relationships today means *greatly increased
responsibility* in relationships.

People who sleep with anyone who comes
along, having sex relationships in an animalistic
way, are going to have a difficult time understanding what a love relationship really is. True
growth with another is a spiritual growth, a
spiritual love. Each person contributes his best
to the other's well-being.

Sex in itself is merely a reciprocation of
energies, one to the other. If this is given in a
spiritual way, the benefits are uplifting and
renewing. Sex should not be abused. If people
misuse their sexual faculties, they will discover
deceit and disharmony growing within them.

In relating to another sexually you are aligning the seven chakras together—whether or not you are consciously aware of this. This is responsible for the energy exchange. Actually an orgasm or lack of orgasm means nothing, because it is the alignment of forces which is the renewing dimension.

Sex, then, should represent a union, an energy exchange, between two souls who are expressing a high love for one another. Such a genuine caring between persons is the key to sexual harmony.

WHAT SPECIFICALLY DO YOU HAVE TO SAY ABOUT MARRIAGE?

A marriage should represent two souls who are loving, working, struggling, playing—and meditating—together. Each is helping the other to work out his or her karmic tasks. It should represent a union in love, a context from which one extends out in love for his fellows.

This, however, must be stressed: couples living together in a state of disharmony, who are unable to grow together, would be better off to go their separate ways. And where there are children involved you must be very careful, for universal laws in this regard are very strong. If a couple decides to divorce legally, all precautions should be taken so that the children will never suffer. So much karma is built because couples *use* children in their own warfare, their own hurts.

If you divorce in harmony, in love and with understanding, simply acknowledging that the two of you are not growing together in a constructive relationship, such may well be the highest course of action.

If you carry bitterness over a break-up, or if you feel hurt, then you must work that out in this incarnation. Otherwise, you will have to come back and work it out with that person in another lifetime. But the biggest debt you will ever pay is when you hurt your children.

WHY DO YOU THINK THERE IS SUCH A RISE IN DIVORCE RATES?

It is very hard to find one mate and continue throughout life with this one and only person. You have much temptation; there are many heavy karmic bonds from past lives. If you understand these things, you can meet them head on when they approach you.

You will be drawn to many people outside your family. You will feel strong emotions you cannot ignore. It is important to understand how to deal with these. If you can love without clinging guilts and shame, love freely and give to others that which you feel is needed—yet without tying yourself to another. Then you will grow, as will the soul whose life you touch. For people will be brought together whose love vibration needs rekindling, who need at that particular moment a reinforcement of self—perhaps it's confidence, perhaps it's understanding, perhaps it is simply tolerance. But you may often be able to lift up the other soul by your sensitivity.

Feeling an intensification of energy, or emotion, toward another does not mean you have to break up a home, get a divorce and remarry. Many times karmic ties, and mutually beneficial relationships, can be established within the context of persons' separate lives.

Let us mention here that often a person feels unhappy with his mate—whether a marriage partner or someone he is living with—when he is unhappy with himself. One's own weaknesses are more apparent in close living situations with others. Trying to avoid a close examination of self, then, may be behind the continuous search for new partners.

This age provides more options for more people. Marriage as traditionally understood is being greatly expanded. People are exploring the meaning of these new possibilities.

HOW DO YOU RELATE THE PROBLEM OF DRUGS TO OUR TIME?

The use of drugs, of course, is nothing new. Man has for centuries known ways to induce states of consciousness far different from that of his normal everyday life. Today drugs are accessible to a much larger number of people. Add this to the frustrations of your society, the desire to find something more meaningful, and you discover that drugs are a convenient way to *escape*. But escape is what they provide— not consciously directed growth.

Whenever you take any drug it sets up a chemical reaction in the physical body. It changes the cellular structure of the bloodstream. If you are using drugs—such as antibiotics—to heal yourself, this may be done to your advantage. However, balance and caution should always be used.

But drugs should never be used in experimentation, for you have no idea of the dangers you may be attracting to yourself. Drugs affect the electro-magnetic field radiating throughout and around the body—they can literally short-circuit this field, and burn it out.

Also, drugs can have the effect of blowing open the energy centers of the body. When this happens you have no control over the forces or entities which may be entering or leaving through these centers. You could become "possessed" by another entity. Because of this radical change your mental state is greatly altered. The forces which may enter your body in this uncontrolled open state may result in schizophrenia, epilepsy, a generally diseased system—and eventually death. You are opening your centers to energy flows that you are not evolved enough to handle—or else they would already be open. It is this energy that burns out the cells in the brain and the body, not the drug itself.

This is why meditation is the only safe way to accelerate the opening of the energy centers, hence gaining new perspectives in consciousness. In meditation you will be given the amount of energy you can safely hold, and you are always in control.

WHAT KIND OF CHANGES ARE NECESSARY IN THE EDUCATIONAL SYSTEM TO MEET THE PROBLEMS OF THE AGE?

Education must eventually rest on the shoulders of the master teachers who know how to guide the individual to the university within. Although objective knowledge about the universe will be more readily obtainable, it is incidental after one has touched deeper levels of being.

Great breakthroughs will be made in rate of learning so that a person may accumulate the necessary knowledge to function in a highly specialized world. But there will be the need to balance the mental man with the emotional, physical, and spiritual man. Education at its

best will move into   dimensional learning. All
the human dimensions will be explored, understood and controlled. You must have a balanced
program of growth—teaching the whole man.
And then great strides will be made in re-
educating people away from war, away from
fear, away from hatred. You must educate your
children to move toward a harmony both without
and within.

▲

Sometimes Betty's teachers give specific
predictions about the age we are presently
living in—about developing trends now and in
the years ahead. They are usually reluctant to
do this, because they believe man has freedom
to make choices which can affect the course of
events. They emphasize that *inner awareness*—
not external happenings—is what ultimately
influences these outer events.

The main   prediction   which *does* consis-
tently channel through Betty is in the form of
a warning: "Turmoil and destruction threaten
your country and your world. The only way to
avoid this violence is to increase dramatically
the pace of spiritual growth."

It is this which gives a note of urgency to
Betty's work.

Chapter Seven

TOWARD A WORLD OF PEACE

It hardly need be emphasized that war and the threat of war in our world is a major cause of anxiety and frustration. The present tragic conflicts mean intense personal suffering for those directly involved, of course. Yet hardly anyone, however remote from the actual fighting, could fail to be moved by the almost daily newspaper pictures of the killed and wounded, the homeless men and women, and the orphaned children.

Why would a supposedly good God, or Cosmic Intelligence, permit apparently innocent people to suffer? Why would such a God permit a seemingly hopeless estrangement among nations?

Not only has Betty experienced the death of her eldest son in the Viet Nam conflict (blown

97

up by a land mine), but she has been called upon by many persons for assistance in facing the death of their loved ones in the war. In addition, she has often counseled young servicemen—many hooked on drugs—who are now trying to readjust to the society at home.

Again and again her guides set our concerns and our questions about war in a larger universal or cosmic perspective. And they rarely fail to emphasize the dimension of individual responsibility: we *can* do something about the present situation; it *is* within our capabilities.

Those who are looking for an external corrective—such as political pressure on governments, United Nations action, and the like—are bound to be disappointed with what comes through Betty. Manipulating outer circumstances is not the way.

Asked specifically, "What is war?" her teachers replied: "War is a result of discord among men who are not at peace with themselves. Man's lack of love for his fellows results in the effort to control others, to exploit others, and to take what is possessed by others. War is the expression of greed, the very opposite of love."

Questioned further, they elaborated: "War represents man's scattered energies, his illusion of separateness from his fellows. War is the negative state of man's creative energy and power. War embodies hostility, hatred, and envy, which are expressions of man's ignorance and misunderstanding."

The outer manifestations of war—manufacturing weapons, destroying vegetation, causing one's fellow human beings great pain and suffering, the actual killing—begin within the individual human being. For war is the expression of the turmoil within individual minds.

"Think of the hostile thoughts that pass through your own consciousness during a single day," reminded Betty. "Hostile vibrations expand into outward reality and we find ourselves saying and doing things hurtful to others. 'As a man thinketh, so is he.' War, the outer manifestation of our inner violence and hatred, can indeed be prevented—but only by persons regulating their individual thought vibrations. War can never be regulated by legislation. The negativity which causes war will only express itself in other ways—angry words, petty jealousies, personal hostilities. And these things are as destructive as the devastation we are accustomed to calling war."

This view is consistent with that of both Eastern and Western traditions which point out that conquering one's self is far more significant than conquering a nation. Unless a man con-

quers himself—his own renegade passions and
greed—he has conquered nothing.

Peace, then, refers to the inner realms of
being. For Betty it represents a state of consciousness attuned to the cosmic consciousness.
This is variously called the inner light, the
Christ light, or the God force within. There is a
very real *level of vibration* that is identified with
peace, ultimately more real and powerful than
the destructive lower vibrations of hostility and
hatred.

Can man ever hope to create a peaceful world?
"Yes, of course," affirmed Betty. "Large numbers of persons expressing the vibrations of love
and peace will bring harmony among men. *But
we have to start with ourselves where the problem has its origin.* We spread it to others, and
they to others, until real peace comes. This is
what makes our work so important."

The following trance message deals not so
much with war as such, but with each man's
potential for the development of the positive
qualities of peace and harmony.

PEACE, BROTHERHOOD, AND HARMONY

You ask us to speak on peace and brotherhood.
We would add "harmony," for without harmony
you cannot develop the other two.

What is peace? Is it outward agreements
among nations, or between neighbors? No, when

people search deeply they discover peace is something which resides in the God-soul. Only when they take time to develop an awareness of peace will they bring this flow of energy into every dimension of their lives.

Without personal peace within the individuals who make up nations, it is not possible for nations to get along with one another. This is important to the success of your own government, your own land. Each of you can learn to feel and to know the peace which resides deep in the soul. If you cannot accomplish this *within* yourself, you will find it cannot exist *without*.

Peace is a blending of persons in truth and harmony, one with the other. It is seeing the God-nature of every man. It is reaching out and extending to every fellow human being the love force you discover at the center of your own nature.

All are essentially one unit. What is needed is a harmonizing of vibrations, the positive vibrations at the love end of the vibratory scale. If each soul were *aware* of the peace-love power within, there would be a natural harmony uniting all men in a brotherhood which could withstand all threats. There would not be war or suffering, for men would be free from the greed and hatred that makes them exploit one another.

If you could accept the plan or will of the one God, the Cosmic Intelligence, you would see that it intends each person to find his identity with the God-source and with all his fellow creatures. You would know that as you hurt another you hurt yourself. And as you give to another you receive in return. This is the law of karma in action. If you would develop the love power, and learn to express it in your daily living, you would find the brotherhood your world is searching for would actually *be*.

How tragic is the lack of trust in your land and among the nations! If peace reigned within your hearts, the sorrow and suffering of discord throughout the world would end. This is our whole task, and yours if you will accept it—to encourage love and peace among men.

The task of all mankind is thus essentially a peace-building task. True peace is the God power or love force manifesting through you as you get in touch with your divine nature. There is no way really to serve mankind other than to bring this love force to its fullest potential within your own being.

In brotherhood you will be able to become fully aware of those less fortunate than yourself. We do not ask that you give to others material things, although if one is starving or needs shelter he should not be turned away. The greatest gift you can impart to your fellow men is the teaching that love and peace can flow from their own meditation. You cannot, of course, do it for them—they must learn it themselves. But you can set them on the path and guide them until such time as they are able to know their own inner strength.

It is sometimes very difficult when one is crying out for help to tell him he must do it himself. It is a big responsibility to *live* and to transmit the higher teachings to others. Yet it is a task made easier if you call upon the love-source for guidance and knowledge.

It is easier to help a person who knows nothing than a wise man who knows all. For those who "know" only on the mental plane will not be able to set aside their intellect in order to *feel* and thus to grow on the deeper levels of awareness. It is the lower self which manifests as the logical intellect of mankind. It is emphasis on this to the exclusion of the higher intuitive or feeling self which has brought your nation to the brink of disaster.

There will be times when you will be called upon to help one who is in need who does not offer peace and love in return. It is still important for you to do all in your power to teach the right attitude and to share the knowledge of how to find the way if one should desire to choose it. Whether the other person accepts what you offer is not your responsibility. It is his choice and his responsibility. Your task is to plant the seed and nurture its growth as fully as possible. But if one chooses not to continue in the way, you must respect his decision and release him to go his way while still continuing to love and care about him.

It is not possible for us to tell you how foolishly people scatter their forces. We see you running hither and yon, throwing your vibrations to the winds. If the energy you are throwing away could be focused to bring about a harmony within, it would radiate a force field of love which would literally attract thousands. In meditation you learn to focus this power.

The inner peace you develop through meditation will shine as a beacon light onto the earth plane as well as in the higher planes. Many on the astral, and even in the higher realms, do not know peace within themselves. If it is found on your earth plane, it is maintained throughout the other spheres.

It is on the earth that you must learn these essential lessons of peace, brotherhood, and harmony. You must pass your tests here, either in this lifetime or another. This growth cannot be readily attained on the other planes. Even though much can be taught on the various levels between incarnations, you must then go back to the earth plane to test and try, to see whether you indeed gained the growth you were striving for.

A total peace throughout its existence on earth —this is exactly what each soul is striving for. That is why you incarnated. If you learn to become one with others and generate the peace vibration, you will have love and peace on every other plane of being. And once the earth test is finally passed, you need not return but may continue on the higher realms of existence.

▲

The message channeled through Betty is a teaching of hope. It is also a teaching that tremendous individual responsibility is required if that hope is to be realized. In essence she is saying: (1) every man can acheive peace—it is open to all; (2) an act of the will and a sustained effort is needed; and (3) the result is the attainment of life at its fullest, a life of love, harmony and brotherhood.

One has free will. He may accept or reject the way to this fullness of life. If he rejects it, he continues to reap disharmony, suffering, and war. He continues to bring the results of such a choice not only to himself but to others. He thus prevents world peace from coming.

But a man may choose the way of peace at any time. He may begin wherever he is. For the

divine love surrounds him always, and resides
within him as an unseen seed, ready to spring to
life the moment he nurtures it ever so little.

If he accepts the opportunity to attain peace
and harmony, he is assured of encouragement
and help from countless entities—on the earth
plane and beyond. He is by no means alone, and
the reward is unimagined joy.

Such appears to be Betty's teaching. And she
asks: "What other way is there?"

Chapter Eight

UNDERSTANDING EMOTIONS

"Emotions run high," an old expression goes. We may be moved to tears in compassion for a fellow human being, or we may violently attack another in a fit of anger, jealousy, or hatred.

The emotional nature of man, according to Betty, can be one's biggest ally or his worst enemy. The key is directing the emotional energy to the God-self within—not directing it outward and scattering your forces. Through questions and answers in a trance session she describes the nature of emotion, how it relates to self love, and how to use the power for your best growth.

107

WHAT ACTUALLY IS EMOTION?

Emotion is a force which is part of the lower
self, being expressed through the lower chakras.
Normally, emotions are expressed through the
third chakra, or solar plexus, in the form of
feeling and sensation. On the "emotional scale"
of man there are both the positive and negative
expressions.

Emotion is the force you must discipline the
most within yourself. Emotions are what lead
people to feel sorry for themselves, or to condemn
others. Emotions can be destructive. For an
undisciplined emotion is like a child who scatters
energy irresponsibly and misuses it. But emotion
may be used as a precious gift, which aids man
in sensing and relating to the beauty and the
oneness in all things.

IS IT WISE TO BLOCK OR HIDE OUR TRUE
EMOTIONAL FEELINGS?

Not from yourself. Blocking the emotions is
not training or disciplining them. The emotional
nature of man is one which must be *experienced.*
Many people believe that by not allowing their
emotions to come out, by hiding within, they
can achieve inner peace. This is not the case.
The emotions must be looked at constructively
and worked through.

BUT ISN'T THIS SOMETIMES PAINFUL?

Opening the emotions means suffering—and growth. For they can steer you toward hatred and fear, or toward deep devotion, trust, and love.

HOW CAN THE EMOTIONAL NATURE—SEEMINGLY SO UNSTEADY—STEER ONE TOWARD "TRUST AND LOVE"?

You may use these emotional feelings as a tool for understanding yourself. Examine these feelings, and see where and why they are directed toward particular people and situations.

Your positive emotions are a bridge to the God-force, to the higher centers in man. When the force of a positive emotion is directed within the self, it may attune you to the inner teachings. You will sense the powerful love force within all souls.

You can, then, learn to use the *emotional* self as a *devotional* self.

WHAT HAPPENS WHEN WE DON'T DIRECT THE EMOTIONAL FORCE WITHIN?

When it is directed outward, or scattered, the energy loss tends to weaken rather than strengthen the person. Hence, envy, jealousy, and passions of various kinds grow in the conscious mind.

BUT WHAT ABOUT TWO PEOPLE
"IN LOVE," EACH DIRECTING ENERGY
TOWARD THE OTHER?

This can be a very powerful exchange of energies, and will have the effect of increased vitality on the persons involved. But if there is a lack of strong self-love in the relationship, centered in the ʼGod-self, what happens when one person suddenly goes his or her separate way? If there is no new person with whom you may exchange energy on this level of intensity, one or both parties feels depleted and depressed.

You may say, "When I feel love for another person I am directing it outward." And we would say, "Unless you first love yourself (directing the force inward) you cannot genuinely love others." (Otherwise, your love for another may rest on insecurity, a need to be accepted—and this is in fact an emotion of fear, not love.)

ISN'T IT POSSIBLE TO GET INVOLVED
IN A BIG EGO TRIP WHEN YOU TRY
TO LOVE YOURSELF?

True self love has nothing to do with being involved in a big ego. It is an acceptance of self—as of all selves—as a child of God. True self love enables you to see all men as fellow growing entities, for once you realize your oneness with the God-force, your perspective becomes more universal. It is not a matter of thinking "I am better than that person," or "I have a better personality than she does." Rather it is knowing that you and all creatures are undergirded by the love of the universe, and that all are working at various stages of development.

If true self love existed there could be no hatred of others. For you would perceive the boundless love of the universe flowing in and through your being. You would be filled with joy and understanding, eager to share this universal love with every other self.

Any negative emotions—hatred, fear, envy—block the realization of this self-love. They thwart your own growth and may hinder your fellows.

YOU MENTION FEAR. HOW CAN MAN
LEARN TO OVERCOME HIS FEARS?

Fear is one of the greatest destroyers of mankind. Both fear and hatred are given their power by the soul itself, by the doubts which creep into you. You may be afraid to face reality, or your own weaknesses. Fear comes from hiding within yourself.

The only way to overcome fear, or the thing you are afraid of, is to confront it directly, understand it, and thus no longer give it the power to exist.

THIS SEEMS TO BE EASIER SAID THAN DONE!

That which you fear you must face. Do not walk away from your fear, but walk up to it with arms outstretched in greeting. To your surprise you will find that in projecting love toward your fear, you will destroy it. For darkness and ignorance cannot survive in the light of love.

In this way you may literally kill your fears, your guilts, and your bad habits. This cannot be too strongly emphasized: *there is a need to confront the very thing you are running from.* Don't put it off until tomorrow, but walk up to it now. And you will no longer have that fear.

WHAT ARE SOME OF THE MOST
MENACING FEARS TODAY?

Fear of failure is one of the biggest blocks which each soul must face. Each of you will make mistakes, but this is not failure.

Related to this is the fear of a hurt ego. When one seeks truth his ego may be badly bruised, for he is having to knock down many of the old confining notions of self and replace them with a cosmic perspective. As the ego falls away, the soul advances.

You must understand that the purpose of life is to grow, to progress—to make mistakes, yet learn from them in order to help your fellows. To accomplish any task set before you, proceed with all your strength of purpose and with a positive attitude. Whatever the outcome, you are giving it the full potential of your creativity. Then, if you should fail in one or more dimensions of the effort, you really have not failed at all. For you have gained strength and knowledge, and this will serve you at a later time.

CAN WE GET HELP IN FACING OUR FEARS?

Your guide, your God, and your own spiritual self will never fail you. The tremendous power which lies within will enable you to meet every challenge.

Remember that a sense of humor is very important in overcoming your fears, your negative emotions. Being able to laugh at one's own mistakes has an uplifting, balancing effect. When you are depressed, very often you fail to see the true lesson you were meant to learn. But if you can laugh and look at the situation lightheartedly, the lesson will shine through— and you can grow through it.

YOU MENTION GUILT. IS GUILT AN
EMOTIONAL RESPONSE?

Yes. Guilt is based on an ignorance of the
universal law of karma. Guilt is rooted in fear,
and must be neutralized or overcome.

WHAT PART DOES THE IDEA OF
FORGIVENESS PLAY HERE?

The traditional view of forgiveness is that
man wants somebody to erase the consequences
of what he does. But nobody can do this for
him. He can, however, effect his own change,
and must accept the responsibility of his actions
and learn from them. The law of karma is a
universal law, and the traditional concept of
forgiveness doesn't make much sense in the
light of it.

Man's desire for forgiveness implies a lack of
trust in the divine power as a loving, caring
force. His search for pardon suggests that he
thinks God is vindictive, and delights in seeing
man suffer. Man is always forgiven, as it
were, even though he must accept the responsibility of his actions. When man feels guilty or
unforgiven it is based on his complete misconception of ultimate reality.

Wanting forgiveness is really a desire for self-
acceptance. What man needs most is to stop
blaming himself, and others.

For the purpose of life is to grow. "Forgiveness" in the scriptures mainly concerns the importance of ridding the self of guilts, hence freeing the self. If one is hung-up in his own guilts, he cannot be aware of the needs of his fellows. You must put these guilts and fears aside, and dwell only on your strengths.

Remember that all people have hurt others, have hated, have acted violently. None are free from the pangs of growth through the earth plane. Thus, as you learn to see yourself as part of the whole human life wave, you feel the struggles, the joys and the frustrations of all people.

You learn to accept the responsibility of your own thoughts, words, and deeds. And you are filled with love and compassion for all men.

It is only by being attuned to the God-force that you can truly correct your deeds. You can keep from hurting others only by being responsive to the God within.

EARLIER YOU INDICATED THAT MAN'S EMOTIONAL NATURE IS PART OF HIS LOWER SELF. DOES THIS MEAN HE CAN HOPE TO GROW BEYOND THE EMOTIONAL STAGE AS HE DIRECTS THIS FORCE INWARD?

Yes, man will grow beyond the stage where his emotions rule him. He will learn to

activate higher chakras. Strength of will is one
of his greatest aids in stabilizing the emotional
nature.

But before he can do this he must express the
emotions, and look at them. By being able to
see them for what they are, he will grow to the
point where they no longer hold sway over his
life. Then he will have directed the emotional
force toward the *higher centers within* through
the strength of his *will*. He will no longer experience the feeling of   separateness.

Chapter Nine

CONCENTRATION
AND
MEDITATION

At the heart of the message that channels through Betty is the process of meditation. "It's nothing new," she is quick to explain. "People have been practicing meditation for thousands of years."

But in the Western world there has been a tendency to regard meditation as something vague and mysterious. People tend to think that it is something appropriate to the monk in the monastery, or to the followers of "strange oriental religions."

That techniques of concentration and meditation could be important to modern life is just beginning to dawn on many thoughtful persons in our culture.

What is meditation and what is its purpose? What are the specific techniques? The problems? The results? Betty feels the answers she has been given to these questions are no better than those of any other system—all forms of meditation are beneficial. But two criteria set her method apart from many others. First, without being naive, it is simple enough for anyone to understand. Second, it is practical in an active lifestyle—it helps people to meet real problems in the here and now.

A booklet on concentration and meditation as Betty teaches it is available from the Inner Light Foundaton. The answers to the specific questions which follow discuss a portion of that material, and add further counsel and elaboration on many points.

WHAT IS MEDITATION?

In simplest terms, meditation is a way of going within, of discovering yourself. It is not a religion, but can enrich any faith. It may be practiced by persons of any religious belief, or by those who have no formal faith whatsoever.

Meditation offers no magic answer to life's problems, nor is it an escape from life. It is not an end in itself; it is a process, a means to an end.

WHAT IS THIS "END" OR PURPOSE OF MEDITATION?

On one level, the purpose of meditation is to develop an inner peace and serenity—to become free of frustration and anxieties, to overcome hostility, to learn to relate more harmoniously with other people, to find clearer direction for your life.

On a deeper level, the purpose of meditation is to get in touch with the God-center of your being—to become more fully aware of the divine spark within yourself and others. This awareness puts you in tune with the powerful unseen energies of the universe. And these forces work with you to help you learn to manifest love and compassion for others.

Meditation, then, leads you to an *inner* knowing, a receptiveness to the deeper meaning of your existence.

YOU MENTION THE "GOD-CENTER"—DOES THIS MEAN ONE HAS TO BELIEVE IN GOD?

Meditation does not depend in any way on what you *believe*. You do not even have to believe in the value of meditation itself! All that is required is a willingness to try it. The religious

skeptic will usually acknowledge some universal energy or cosmic process. He will
grant that every person must in some way be
a result or expression of such an energy or
process—it is somehow within or inherent in
each one. Meditation is the way to make contact
with this creative force. You may call it whatever you wish. We call it God.

WHY DO YOU SPEAK OF BOTH CONCENTRATION
AND MEDITATION—ARE THEY TWO
DIFFERENT THINGS?

Actually, they are two parts of the total
process we call meditation. Concentration is the
directed mental effort that precedes meditation.
In concentration you quiet the mind and
consciously focus it on something. In meditation
you aren't trying to focus on anything, but are
allowing a free-flowing reception.

WHAT ARE THE SPECIFIC TECHNIQUES
AS YOU TEACH THEM THROUGH BETTY?

We offer a plan requiring about twenty
minutes a day. First, you need a quiet place
where you will not be disturbed. Before you
begin you should spend a few moments reading
something inspirational, such as poetry, religious
writings, or perhaps listening to uplifting

music. This will help set the tone for your meditation period.

Choose a comfortable sitting position. It does not matter how you sit, so long as the spine is straight. Many will find that the most comfortable position is in a straight back chair, with spine erect and feet flat on the floor. We suggest you place your hands folded together in your lap, or with palms gently touching and fingertips together. And for this first stage—concentration—your eyes may be either open or closed.

Now focus your attention on one word, one symbol, a picture, a feeling, perhaps a soft light. Or, you might use a sound, as in a mantra or holy chant. But whatever you choose, it should be *only one thing* for the duration of the concentration period—and it should be something which has inspirational or symbolic importance for you personally. It should suggest qualities like beauty, joy, love, and peace.

If your eyes are open during concentration, you should be focusing on the object you have chosen. Hold this image to the best of your ability for the full ten minutes. And whenever your mind wanders, gently draw it back and continue.

Simple as it appears, this process will build energy and help bring together the physical, the mental, and the spiritual into one harmonious vibration. Without realizing it you will be feeding the inner spirit and preparing the way for the next phase which is to follow.

COULD YOU BE MORE SPECIFIC ABOUT THE MENTAL IMAGERY DURING CONCENTRATION?

Let us point out again that the purpose of this imagery is to *discipline* your thoughts—and point them toward the highest ideal (such as beauty, joy, love). In order to be receptive to the inner stillness, you must learn to control, to quiet, the many thoughts which dart through your mind and scatter your attention. By focusing on a single idea or picture, you are providing the mind an anchor—to hold the thought energy steady.

For an example, you may take the image of a red rose, symbolizing love. In your mind's eye you would see this rose in all its delicate loveliness. You might breathe its fragrance, sense the softness of each perfectly formed petal. You become totally absorbed in the idea and picture of the rose. Nothing else enters your thoughts at all.

Or, if you are in the Christian tradition you might choose a cross. You would focus on this symbol—either looking at a cross with your eyes

SUGGESTED CONCENTRATION POSITION: SPINE
ERECT, EYES CLOSED OR OPEN, FEET FLAT ON
FLOOR, HANDS TOGETHER.

open or seeing a cross in your mind with eyes closed. Again, you would direct all your attention to the beauty and meaning of the cross—no other thoughts would be allowed to intrude.

Your own creativity will present countless ways of holding and intensifying various concentration symbols.

HOW DOES ONE MOVE TO THE MEDITATION STAGE?

After about ten minutes of the concentration, or when it feels right, just turn the hands over, palms up, and let them rest gently on your lap. Continue to sit in the same posture.

Now you release your mind from its controlled attention on the concentration symbol. Put it in neutral and permit thoughts to flow. You are still, or passive. But you are also alert, fully aware of what is happening. You are in a state of passive awareness. You might pretend you are watching a motion picture, letting it progress, not trying to hold it.

This free-flowing receptiveness is a time of listening and learning. The inflowing is likely to come in pictures or images; to some it comes in feelings, or even through voices. It could come in the form of new ideas that seem to just pop in. Or, you could feel a sense of increased energy. However it comes, accept it as your

SUGGESTED MEDITATION POSITION: SPINE ERECT, EYES CLOSED, FEET FLAT ON FLOOR, PALMS TURNED UP.

deeper, inner self coming into your conscious awareness.

But don't be disturbed if you think you aren't getting anything. Experiencing the peacefulness of this receptive state always helps align the forces of the self, and heighten your vibrations. It is the daily practice over an extended period of time that helps bring results.

HOW IS THIS STAGE BROUGHT TO A CONCLUSION?

Again, not by watching a clock, but by your inner timing. Ten minutes is a kind of minimum. Remain for as long as thirty to forty minutes if your schedule permits and the process continues to be productive.

When it feels right to end the session, you need to close off the vivid receptiveness by a conscious effort. In your mind picture yourself surrounded by a white or gold light—which symbolizes truth. Or you may picture a huge white balloon, and yourself stepping into its center.

The reason for this closing down is not to shut off your receptiveness to your inner teacher, nor to shut out your concern and caring for others. Rather it is providing you with a protected sensitivity. It prevents you from being adversely affected by other people's negative vibrations. If you fail to close down or protect yourself, another person's anxiety could make you anxious, or another's depression make you depressed—without your realizing what was happening.

This closing down is a protective shield with a double purpose: to keep out unwanted influences, and to retain the positive outcomes of the meditation flow. (You may use this technique at any time you feel you are being adversely affected by others, or are experiencing a low energy level.)

As long as meditation was confined to the quiet life of the monastery this precaution was unnecessary. But more and more persons are now being exposed to the mystical teachings, and the resulting heightened awareness makes it absolutely essential that a person protect himself from the countless disturbing vibrations in noisy everyday life.

WHAT ARE SOME OF THE RESULTS OF MEDITATION?

Very simply, the transformation of the self. Almost without realizing it and over a period of time, you will become a different person. The undesirable aspects of yourself—worry, sense of worthlessness, hostile attitudes, bad habits and so on—will gradually fade away. They will be replaced by confidence, joy, love, self-control, a sense of meaning and purpose in life.

You begin to know who you are—a spark of the divine nature. You begin to learn how to manifest this nature in compassion toward your fellows.

No two persons will have exactly the same results, however, for each person's needs are unique. You have incarnated, each of you, to work out specific problems in your present lifetime. You may expect meditation to put you in touch with your task and to help you advance toward its fulfillment.

HOW FAST CAN THESE RESULTS BE EXPECTED?

Everyone has free will and may be expected to move at his own pace. But some positive benefits will be experienced almost immediately—the peacefulness during the meditation period itself, and the good feeling that you are on your way to accelerated growth.

Very soon, however, you will discover that people and situations which formerly made you up tight don't bother you as much. You are inclined to be more understanding toward others. You are thinking more about your own life's meaning and direction.

You may hardly be aware of these day by day changes. But over a month, six months, a year, tremendous change will result.

ARE THERE PROBLEMS A PERSON NEEDS
TO KNOW ABOUT?

Rightly understood and sensibly practiced, meditation cannot possibly be dangerous or harmful. It can only result in the good, for the whole orientation or direction is toward the love force, or goodness power in the universe.

But, of course, there are pitfalls. You may not see results as rapidly as you wish, get discouraged, and give up. Or you could go on an ego trip —thinking you're better than others because you meditate regularly. (In orthodox religious groups this is called the "sin of spiritual pride.")

Some people experience unusual sensations they do not understand, and so they become frightened. Perhaps it is a sudden rush of energy up the spine, the feeling of a breeze on your face, or tingling in your hands. But when you become fearful, you may open yourself to the immediate seeing of the results of this fear in a grotesque thought vibration. This could be from your own thoughts, or from lower entities around you who are aware of your fear.

If you ever see anything bad, or frightening, you can simply close your palms and open your eyes—this breaks the flow immediately. Or while remaining in the meditation state, you may say to the thought form or entity (however you wish to address it): "Go to progression." You are actually saying, "Go on, progress to a higher level; I do not accept you on the fear-producing level."

You can, of course, address your guides directly. Ask them to help you understand the experience, and acknowledge that they are surrounding you in the protective light of truth—you are free from all harm, all fear.

Remember, you are always in control. You can at any time break the meditation flow. If, for example, you begin to rock gently back and forth, your guides are sending you energy to raise your vibrational rate. But if the rocking becomes too great, or you have a slight feeling of nausea, just say, "That's enough for now. Ease it off." (Do not allow this rocking during concentration—only during meditation.)

Also, remember that when you first begin— at least the first several years—meditation should be done in moderation with your every- day living. Meditating too much and too long and possibly neglecting your karmic tasks, will not result in the kind of growth you expect. What you learn in short meditation periods should be tested in your daily life. Meditation is the key to help you be more effective in living, not *escape* from your duties because you have to go meditate.

ARE THERE RULES FOR MEDITATION? SUCH AS, HOW OFTEN? BEST TIME OF DAY?

Guiding principles may be adapted to your personal situation. How often? The answer is daily and regularly. Planning your daily schedule in advance will allow ample and unhurried time. And normally it is best to meditate when you are alert—not right after a big meal, or when you are very tired.

Some will find the early morning hours best—before starting the day you put yourself in tune with your highest principles to help guide you. Others will prefer the evening—right before going to bed. This will put you in a receptive frame of mind for the amazing growth and healing that can occur during sleep.

Ideally, you would spend a few minutes in both the morning and evening. Any other times during the day you happen to think of it, you might take about thirty seconds to say, "I welcome the power of love flowing into my being, and I am at one with my fellow-men." Moments are important in developing a totally new kind of awareness. But for the actual meditation periods, your own life style will determine your choice of time of day.

WHY DO YOU ENCOURAGE MEDITATION GROUPS?

The oneness you share within your groups provides needed encouragement. As you support

one another in love, sharing your feelings,
problems, and concerns, you will all advance
more rapidly and with a deeper joy and sense
of fulfillment. Unity with the divine depends
in part upon unity with your brothers.

It is easy to feel a sense of *aloneness* if you
are not related to a group. And it is easy to
become discouraged and to give up. The group
is like an anchor. It is a concrete manifestation
of the divine caring for each person's growth,
and its very existence is a source of reassurance.
It is a vehicle for helping others, especially
newly awakening seekers. Thus it is the vehicle
through which you give and receive help.

WHAT IS THE RELATIONSHIP BETWEEN MEDITATION AND HEALING?

Healing is a complex process. In general it
involves bringing about vibrational harmony
among all aspects of the self—spirit, mind, and
body. Meditation is an attunement process, and
thus it is also a healing process.

People who seriously undertake meditation
are likely to experience an increase in vitality
and a general improvement in health. Specific
symptoms are likely to disappear.

People who meditate regularly may soon
feel an energy flow from their fingertips—which
is the healing power. They will learn to become

channels through which this healing energy can flow to their fellows. In meditation groups this healing power may be greatly multiplied. It may be directed to a member of the group or to someone absent.

Do not hesitate to send out healing thoughts, even if you think you are not sufficiently developed to do so. Vividly *picture* the patient well and active, the healing power of love surrounding him. (This should be done during the concentration period—you are concentrating on a healthy image of the patient.) Then during the free-flowing meditation you release this image, and continue in your free-flowing receptivity. As you finish your concentration-meditation process, quietly thank the healing entities around you for using you as a channel of healing.

It is important to remember that to maintain health—even after a healing —you must meditate to keep your total self in alignment. Otherwise, the same forces which caused the disease in the first place will again manifest themselves.

IS MEDITATION A WAY TO DEVELOP PSYCHIC ABILITY—SUCH AS TELEPATHY OR CLAIRVOYANCE?

Psychic abilities and the experiencing of psychic phenomena are often intensified through meditation. And this is a normal result of

raising your vibrational level—you may at first
be tapping the astral realm, which is beyond
the time-space world. But if your purpose of
meditation is just to gain psychic power, ask
yourself, "Why do I want these powers?" Will
they help you grow in love and awareness?
Will they help you serve others?

What you are striving for in meditation goes
much beyond the psychic realm. If you stop
and get side-tracked with psychic ability, you
will not meet your goal of cosmic consciousness,
the expansion your soul seeks.

It is our counsel that you should not make
the development of these gifts the *purpose* of
your meditation. But if they do come, welcome
them and dedicate them to the divine power. Ask
your spirit teachers to guide you in using them
wisely, never to show off or to gain power
over others.

WHAT IS THE PLACE OF FAITH IN MEDITATION?

There are many levels of awareness higher
than your own. What seems to you inconsistent
and bewildering may have a reason in the total
scheme of the universe. Faith is the confidence
that although you may not at present understand many things, you are daily discovering
more and more. It is the confidence that your
spirit guides and the universal cosmic power

are working together for your good and the good of all men.

This inner knowing called faith is *real*—it is a vibration of peaceful direction. As you learn to trust it you are led into new growth experiences.

IS MEDITATION IN ANY WAY RELATED TO SLEEP?

The spiritual masters have long known that the more time they spent in meditation, the less sleep they needed. The physical body needs sleep to rejuvenate and rebuild itself, to relax tension and to have a reprieve from the conscious mind. But this process is accelerated if body, mind, and spirit are first harmonized through meditation—thirty minutes of meditation may substitute for two or three hours of sleep.

Physical sleep alone will not replenish the energy needed for the harmonious working together of the physical-mental-spiritual self. If worry and fear prevent you from relaxing, you will wake up tired the next morning. This is one reason that meditation just before bedtime is helpful. You attune all aspects of yourself so that your whole being may be renewed, and that you will be more receptive to the teaching you receive during sleep.

The soul, the real you, does not need physical sleep. Consequently, when the body is at rest, *you* are taken from the body and taught on the higher planes. Your teachers give you insight about how to meet the forthcoming situations in your life, particularly those of great stress. When you awake you may not consciously remember what you have been taught, but what you have learned is available to you and may be drawn upon when needed by the conscious mind. In meditation you are actually aware of these teachings—listening to them and participating in the process. And the farther along you go in meditation, the easier it will be for you to remember your sleep experiences as well.

The principle is simple. As you fall asleep your etheric self leaves the body on the level of your immediate mental state. If you have spent that last half hour in meditation, you will go out on a much higher level than if you have spent it watching a horror movie!

WHEN YOU SPEAK OF LEAVING THE BODY ON DIFFERENT LEVELS, ARE YOU REFERRING TO THE ENERGY CENTERS OR CHAKRAS WITH THE VARYING VIBRATIONAL RATES?

Yes, the chakra from which you leave will determine the quality of the perceptions and learning. You will have quite a different experience if you leave through the second chakra than if you leave through the "third eye" or crown chakra. Meditation raises the energy level to the higher chakras. Reading inspirational materials will also help to lead you to a higher plane.

IS THIS LEAVING THE BODY DURING SLEEP THE SAME THING AS "ASTRAL PROJECTION"?

Astral projection would mean travel or experiencing on the astral plane. This is the vibrational level closest to the physical level. To receive the *higher* teachings you must go to higher levels, what may be called the celestial realms and beyond. "Higher plane projection" would be a better terminology.

DO YOU ADVISE THE EXERCISES SOME PEOPLE TEACH FOR THIS OUT-OF-BODY TRAVEL?

We must offer a warning at this point. People may practice specific exercises to enable them to leave the body. But if they do not understand the whole principle of spiritual growth and that what you experience depends on the level you get to—they may have some very bad experiences. In a way it's like giving a child a match to play with. If you don't understand it, it can be a dangerous tool—and risky karmically. Too many people seek the experience solely for the thrill, without understanding the significance of the vehicle for spiritual growth.

When you are ready, your guide will slip you out of the body—it's that simple. But you should work on your spiritual development, attuning to higher and higher energies. Then, when it is right, you will be able to leave freely under proper direction and guidance.

HOW DOES ALL THIS RELATE TO DREAMING?

Dreams play a vital part in developing spiritual awareness. Primitive man understood his dreams as the self actually leaving the body and having those experiences he dreamed about. And he was not entirely mistaken. In most dreams one is not *literally* having the experience, but the dream is the symbolic representation of a process which is occurring within one or more levels of consciousness.

This process involves the superconscious (the universal force, the God-power) feeding into the subconscious (the hidden levels of self) the teachings and experiences needed for enhanced spiritual insight. The life problems you are facing are being worked out through your dreams.

DO DREAMS TAKE THE PLACE OF ACTUAL KARMIC EXPERIENCES?

Not in a way that you could properly understand, although many things—or directions— are worked out on the dream level. It is possible—but rare—that two souls living in the body will be allowed to work out their karmic ties in their dreaming while both are still on the earth plane. Perhaps it is impossible for them to ever physically see one another again. But while out of the body, in the dream state, they will meet, embrace, forgive and love one another.

ARE THERE ANY CENTRAL GUIDING PRINCIPLES REGARDING MEDITATION WHICH YOU CAN LEAVE WITH US?

Yes, and no doubt you've heard them all your life and will not at first grasp their profound importance.

They are simply "God is love" and "Do unto others as you would have them do unto you."

Let these principles shape your concentration period, and ask the higher powers to open their meaning to you in the receptiveness of the meditation period. Everything else is simply an elaboration of these teachings.

Meditation is often difficult for people at first. It requires self-discipline and a creative imagination. One form of imagery Betty suggests may be appropriate in conclusion.

Perhaps you are having a hard time getting the hang of this free-flowing receptiveness in the meditation period. If this is the case, right

after the concentration period, imagine yourself
walking up to a cascading waterfall, which is
among lush growth in a peaceful and beautiful
setting. You pause to rest and refresh yourself.
As you relax, your spirit guide approaches. He
(or she—whichever you prefer) walks up to
you, and seems to have the "wisdom of the ages"
written on his face. A great power of love
emanates from your guide to you—and you are
filled with joy.

Then he begins to speak, and you know he
understands your deepest need. Listen to what
he is saying—carefully. (You will actually *hear*
words of counsel. Don't worry about whether
you are making them up.) When the period
of teaching is over, he quietly disappears from
the waterfall scene, and you continue to reflect
on his words. As you open your eyes and end
the meditation period, you know that your guide
is still with you, and that you will never have
to feel frightened or alone.

The process of actually picturing your guide
talking with you is one way to develop the
meditation flow. But remember there are many
methods, and many techniques are available,
especially through Hindu and Buddhist writings.
Betty's guides would not reject any method
that genuinely contributed to a person's development. They affirm that all meditation is the
same—find the form that feels right for you.

Chapter Ten

THREE CHANGED
LIVES

Thousands of people have come into contact with Betty during the last several years, either through her lectures, radio and television programs, healing groups, meditation groups, or private readings.

So it was not hard to find persons who felt their lives had been transformed through hearing and practicing the message. This chapter reports briefly the stories of three such persons.

"Be sure you make it clear *I* didn't do it," Betty insisted. "We were led together and they opened up and found their own way. They gave me as much as I gave them."

The three themselves also stressed that what they opened up to was responsible for their transformation—not just their own personal effort. Something greater than the normal conscious awareness was guiding them in joyous new dimensions of living.

THE STORY OF MIKE

Soon after his induction into the Army, Mike was on his way to Viet Nam. The day he arrived, word came that his mother had been killed in an automobile accident. He was crushed with grief, and became greatly depressed.

As time stretched on, he found companionship, understanding and love through a new relationship with a Vietnamese girl. She eventually lived with Mike as his wife. One day she stepped on a land mine and was killed.

Again his bereavement soared. He threw himself into his work as a medic, trying to forget the violent deaths of the two people who had meant the most to him. But how could he? For eighteen months he watched the suffering of the war-ravaged Vietnamese, saw his buddies killed and maimed, and found himself narrowly escaping death on more than one occasion.

"Sure, I was high on pot a lot of the time, and I got strung out on both heroin and speed," he acknowledged.

Then he found himself home on leave with an inheritance from his mother of $33,000. All at once he was out of the hell of Viet Nam and could do anything he wanted. He should go back again to what he'd just been through? No chance. He decided to go AWOL.

He soon made new friends —who were interested only in his money. He then found himself ripped off for virtually the full amount.

It was at this point that a girl friend—one of the few who really cared about Mike instead of his money—suggested he get a reading from Betty. Reluctantly Mike agreed. It was right after Betty's own son had been killed in Viet Nam. Her heart immediately went out to the skeptical Mike, who admitted he wanted nothing to do with "fortune-tellers."

In the reading Mike was counseled to turn himself in and face the consequences. All right —what did he really have to lose? After being taken into custody, he came down with hepatitis—and was diagnosed as having psychotic tendencies as well. He was put in a military hospital, which proved to be more than he could handle. Soon Mike escaped, going AWOL again, and tried to return to his old ways. But this time he was out of money and his "friends" had disappeared.

Mike was seriously contemplating suicide when his friend who had previously taken him to Betty suggested he see her again. He agreed, and after a long talk Betty invited him to stay with her family and help them for a while. She would see that he got psychiatric care and get him off drugs. He, in turn, must work toward facing the authorities again. Betty and other Foundation members worked with him daily, providing a source of constant encouragement.

He was suspicious, because he just couldn't believe someone really cared about *him*.

Others were meditating, so Mike found himself trying it, too. It seemed to help more than anything else he tried. And the day came when he was ready to report to the military. Then followed the stockade (where he started a meditation group!), a medical discharge, and finally the freedom to reconstruct his life.

At the time of this writing he has been out of the service for less than three months. Already he is entirely off drugs. He is beginning through meditation and the friendship of fellow seekers to reflect upon the meaning of life. He recalls several accidents in which he had been miraculously unhurt. He remembers out-of-the-body experiences he had largely ignored. He thinks of many instances of divine guidance not recognized at the time.

Where to now for Mike? He doesn't know. But he knows he is in touch with deeper levels of his being than he's ever touched before. He is sure that whatever next steps he takes he will choose responsibly from the context of his new life perspectives.

THE STORY OF JUDY

"Before I met Betty I was what you'd call a thoroughgoing behaviorist," says Judy. "I didn't believe in God. I didn't believe in free will—I thought everything was predetermined in a mechanistic cause-and-effect way. Purpose of life? That question had no meaning. You just lived your life the best you could and took what came. That's all you could do."

Judy hadn't had an easy life. She was left in her early thirties with six children to support. With a family the size of hers she needed to earn extra money to supplement her income as a psychiatric technician at the state hospital. Judy decided to attend a business meeting held by a local distributor to learn more about a new product she might sell part time. The distributor was Betty's husband, and the meeting was to be held at the Bethards' home.

"At the time I'd never heard of Betty—had no idea who she was. I sat through the business meeting, learned a little about Betty, and enjoyed just being in the house.

"I left Betty's house to go to work on the 11:00 p.m. shift at the hospital. About half way there I began to have sharp pains in the back of my neck and a heavy feeling in my chest that made it hard to breathe. My head began to ache intensely. Nothing like this had ever happened to me before, and I guess I was pretty scared. But I drove on for quite a while.

"Suddenly an absurd thought popped into my head: 'Why are you driving this way when you should be driving the other way?' I was driving the right way—where did such a crazy notion come from? I was right at a service station, and I swung in and turned around. Instantly the headache disappeared. I started back toward Betty's. The heavy feeling in my chest disappeared. Another 10 or 15 miles, and the pain in the back of my neck suddenly left.

"As I got to Novato I realized I didn't know where Betty lived. Another girl had ridden there with me and had shown me the way. I hadn't paid much attention to the directions. Here I was, out in the country past midnight, and thoroughly lost. 'To hell with it, I'm going home,' I told myself. I turned around and started back. Then I passed a street that seemed familiar. I turned back again and presently found myself pulling up in front of Betty's house—feeling like an absolute idiot.

"I walked up to the front door and sheepishly announced my presence. 'I don't know what I'm doing here,' I said. 'I hope you do.' Betty laughed. She didn't seem the least bit surprised. 'Hi,' she said, and invited me in, remarking that I 'sure must have strong guides.' I had never heard of guides and had no idea what she was talking about.

"We just talked . . . about the house and how their family had been led to it, and how skeptical I was, how skeptical Betty herself had been.

There was nothing in particular that Betty said or did. She just reassured me that I was in control and didn't need to be afraid because of what had happened. She suggested I get into a meditation group and begin to try to tap some deeper levels of self.

"I did—the very next week. I had never meditated before. I had worked at 'desensitizing' at the hospital—a form of relaxation where you concentrate on relaxing the entire body. But in desensitizing you don't ask questions, seek answers, and invite the mind to flow freely as in meditation. As a behaviorist, I knew there was no place to seek answers from. Being relaxed just meant you were reducing tension so you wouldn't be so up-tight about things.

"Meditation was different. I began to see colors, then scenes and people. My entire life began to change. Answers to my hardest questions began to come, and it seemed I'd really found an 'inner teacher.'

"That was eight months ago and frankly I don't even know the person I was before—she's a complete stranger to me. The person I am now is a brand new person. Life has a meaning and it has a purpose, both of which I never dreamed possible.

"It seems inconceivable to me now that I had actually tried suicide three times, that life was worthless and death a nothingness. I wanted

to die just to get away from it all. I had six
children and a job helping people. But that
hadn't been enough.

"I have experienced a complete reversal of
values. Things I thought were important have
become unimportant; things I thought unimportant are now vitally important. I have a
higher energy level. I have been virtually free
of sickness. I know I have a long way to go,
but I'm on my way and life is wonderful."

THE STORY OF RAY

A talented young art student working toward
his master's degree at the University of Wiscon-
sin, Ray decided to drop out of school. His
mother had been seriously ill, and soon she
passed away. Somehow it didn't seem right to
go back to school then. He had no responsibilities, no motivation, no direction. His under-
graduate major in philosophy had satisfied his
keen intellect at the time, but had provided no
anchor on which to build a purposeful life.

Ray decided to go to California to visit an
old girl friend. He stayed with her for a year
and a half, during which time he had what would
be considered a nervous breakdown.

"I seemed to lose rapport with the environment outside myself," Ray reports. "Here you
are an adult mind and you come to the realization you've lost contact with at least 50 per
cent of your relationship with external reality.

You don't realize how important it is until you've lost it!"

In the midst of this disassociation the one thing to which Ray could still relate was books. He could still read and assimilate ideas even though his functional ability was severely limited. It was at this point that Ray discovered and read his first book about Edgar Cayce.

Prior to this time he had had no interest in the psychic. The mystical he had respected, but had made no effort to participate in it. Now the intellect, the conceptual ability which had always held him in rigid control, had crumbled. For the first time in his life he was wide open to the intuitive, feeling dimension of self.

"New ideas and possibilities struck deep inside, because my intellectual filters and controls were temporarily wiped out," Ray reminisces. "I pursued this new interest even though it was frightening at the time. And slowly a new synthesis of self began to come."

Ray saw a newspaper article about Betty lecturing at the Church of Ignacio and decided to go. He had explored transcendental meditation a little. All his adult life he had held people who meditated in high regard, but didn't think there was anything in it for himself.

From Betty, Ray learned another technique of meditation, and caught an unexpected motivation to get involved. He became a key person in organizing groups throughout the San Francisco area. Looking back in retrospect across the past year, he reflects: "I see now that I have been following my pathway ever since I incarnated . . . I just hadn't realized there was a path there. Now it all falls into place. What meditation does for me is to create an environment in which I am able to see the unfolding of my life in the most constructive, efficient, and fully aware fashion. I've had no dramatic manifestations, just a developing sensitivity that infuses itself throughout all of life."

Ray no longer considers himself to be a disoriented person, out of touch with others. The change, he feels, is entirely a result of his new awareness of the psychic and spiritual realms through the practice of his daily meditation. For it is meditation, he explains, "which produces the effect of purpose, of excitement, of direction, and of continuing growth."

▲

Betty has an unfailing faith in people—and with good reason. Every day brings evidence of changed lives. She never ceases to marvel at the growth both in herself and others.

"The times are ripe," she says, "and many are looking for the way to become renewed persons. Meditation provides the way."

Chapter Eleven

THE PROCESS
OF HEALING

Early in her development Betty was led into
a healing role. This has been a continuing activ-
ity which she has tried to understand on two
levels. First, what is the nature of disease?
Second, what is the process which leads to
healing?

She has also struggled with the problem of
her *task as healer* in contrast to her *task as
teacher*. She realizes now that the two are combined—through her healing she teaches, and
through her teaching she heals. Perhaps her
healing is an example of the message which
comes through her, affirming its essential
soundness and pointing to new dimensions for
everyone who takes the message seriously.

"You too can heal, both yourself and others,"
Betty suggests, *"as you begin to understand the
causes of disease and the process of healing."*

She would be the first to admit the problem
is complex. For example, an illness may be
karmic in nature, brought on by action in
previous lifetimes. Does this mean one can do
nothing about it, except somehow learn to endure
it?

No, for Betty the way of the universe is the
way of health. One has freedom to break out of
the karmic prison house, freedom to reverse
the processes that produced disease, freedom to
choose and to practice the way of health.

When asked, her guides explained that
"disease is a condition brought about by a lack
of harmony within the spiritual, mental or physical self. There would be no disease if people
could keep the rate of vibration of all three
going as a balanced whole. Disease is a mal-
function, a disharmony, of the vibrations."

And how does her healing process fit into
this view of disease? "Healing involves the
changing of the vibratory rate of whichever
element of the self is out of harmony. All three
aspects must be brought together in unified
alignment."

"However," Betty pointed out, "if the person
is not doing daily meditation, not himself

working to keep the vibrations aligned, he's just going to become sick again."

Healing, then, is not a kind of magic which erases all karma and permits a person to go on living just as before. *Healing is a continuing process.* Maintaining a state of good health is permeated with individual responsibility.

The following is a trance message on healing which Betty received in the summer of 1971.

PART ONE

Spiritual healing is a way of bringing into harmony the forces within the body—spiritual, mental and physical. When these are brought together there can be no such thing as disease.

Mankind develops disease through emotional upheaval, mental strain, spiritual blindness, and abuse of the physical vehicle. Each person has been allowed free will to do with his own body as he sees fit. Rarely do people use wisely and without abuse the body which has been given them.

We attempt, as channels of the God-force, to bring about a balancing and an uplifting of the forces within the entity. As the total person is brought into harmony, that which is causing the suffering is corrected.

You, as we, are merely channels through which the healing power is able to flow. It is through the patient's own response, his own effort and openness, that the healing will be made manifest. Neither we nor you can violate a person's free will and force healing upon him.

You ask why healing efforts work on some and not on others? It is not necessarily that you have failed; it may be that the patient is blocking the healing by neglecting to rid himself of the conditions which have brought about the illness. With effort on his part—daily meditation, correct diet, proper exercise, and the blending of his own forces—healing will result.

Actually, there are many factors involved, some of them too complex for man to understand in his present state of development. At times there is an imbalance between the channel and the patient—as a channel of healing you must be in rapport with the patient being treated. Through love and compassion you find the ability to adjust your vibratory rate to that of the patient in order to assist in bringing about a healing result.

This can be understood if you will imagine the blending together of musical chords. You must be synchronized as one. This is the same method we use to blend our vibrations with yours. With practice you learn to raise or lower your vibrations to blend sympathetically with those of the patient. Then we can use you as a channel, a kind of pipeline, to carry the

current to the patient and to elevate the part of
him which is out of harmony, thus bringing
about the needed correction.

This will not, however, cause a spontaneous
cure unless the person has the necessary good
karma and the healing is intended. *It will
accelerate healing, alleviate pain, and reduce
concern over one's condition.* But such healing
energy may not be lasting and will probably
need to be renewed every five to seven days for
the accelerated pace to continue.

If a person is growing as he should, taking
over responsibility for his own healing and
asking the Divine Power for help, he will
discover that he can and will improve, karma
permitting. He will become healthy quickly or
slowly, as free will permits.

Bring to the patient responsibility for his
own healing. Help him learn that all aspects of
himself must be developed and blended together
as one. It is important for him to realize his
responsibility is not just to receive. He too must
work at it in order to accept the healing being
channeled to him.

There are many kinds of healers, but it doesn't
matter in the long run which channel is being
used. For the channel only assists and accel-
erates. It is finally up to the good karma and the
responsiveness of the patient. When he is himself

sensitive and open it is easier to bring about a complete cure in a shorter period of time. By effort, by meditation and by faith the healing can and will endure.

PART TWO

The love vibration is essential to the healing effort. As you develop within your being the divine love, what some would call the Christ love, you will be able to pour or channel into the patient a greater intensity of vibrations.

There is not, however, any way of bringing about a healing if the present illness is God's way of sending the entity back home —what you so mistakenly call death.

You must understand that there has to be a way to take the soul to his spiritual "homeland" in which his growth will continue and from which he will in due time incarnate again on the earth plane. This sometimes is accomplished through an accident or through an illness which is intended to accelerate the patient's spiritual growth. And it cannot be changed by your healing efforts.

Does this mean you should try to judge which is a person's final illness and withhold healing in such a case? No, not at all. Remember that healing is basically an outpouring of the vibration of love. And such efforts will give a person a sense of support and a feeling of acceptance as he pases over to the other side. The power he has been given will sustain him until he reaches the plane he is to reside upon for a while.

In most cases, of course, people are allowed a healing, frequently a complete and permanent healing. But, as we have said before, the illness will return unless the patient accepts responsibility and begins to *change the conditions which brought about the illness in the first place.*

As you grow and develop as a channel of healing, you will find many different ways of directing the healing power. Follow what you instinctively feel.

Lay your hands on the patient if you feel so directed, and in the manner and on the area to which you feel led. If two of you (or more) are working together as healers, it is best to sit facing one another on either side of the patient—rather than sitting side by side. Or if the patient is lying down, you may find it best for one to be at the head and the other at the foot of the patient. The vibrations from your polarity will magnify the healing power, and you will get more cooperation from the patient and faster results. See what ways of sitting or standing in relation to the patient will best produce this polarity which increases the healing power.

As you participate in this process, you will be developing your own ability as channels.

▲

Betty's guides have taught her the technique of etheric surgery, a somewhat rare healing method which she has used with remarkable effectiveness on a number of occasions. Essentially, it involves her being used as a channel to transmit healing to the ailing part of the patient's energy field, or etheric body. It is not necessary for her to touch the physical body at all. (The etheric body is invisible to most people, because of its higher rate of vibration. Recently serious scientific researchers have been probing the nature of this energy body which interpenetrates the dense physical form.)

What about the healing efforts of the physician? Is Betty suggesting that the spiritual healing described here should bypass or preclude the work of the medical doctor?

No, for she herself has a deep respect for the dedicated doctor, and is currently working with both psychiatrists and physicians who are themselves open to the dimensions of spiritual healing. She knows there are many methods of healing. But the most effective and permanent are those which attempt to go to the basic causes and to re-direct the life-style of the total person by the principle of love.

Healing, for Betty, is a kind of special "bonus" which results from the overall effort to attune one's self with the divine and to be an instrument of the love force. It is one of the ways we can clearly see the God-power at work in the world. It is one of the ways we can reach out and help our fellow man.

"Try it!" urges Betty. "It'll make you grow— fast! But don't forget it's got to flow out of a deep love and your daily meditation."

Chapter Twelve

THE UNIVERSE
AND YOU

Every person sooner or later finds himself asking the seemingly unanswerable questions of life. They have been asked and dealt with by all the great religions of the world, and debated among philosophers of various traditions. Some of these are:

What is the meaning of existence?

How may God, or the universal intelligence, be described?

How can I know what is real in a changing and temporary world?

Can I ever understand the nature and purpose of the universe?

Who and what am I?

It is not surprising that people should want to ask the entities which speak through Betty some of these persistent questions. Nor should it disturb us if the answers are less than fully satisfying—perhaps because of our own limited capacity to understand.

Betty has never studied philosophy or theology. And this, she believes, might "make me a better channel than if I already had knowledge which might distort the message." She is interested in probing these areas further. She wants to see to what extent she can receive intelligible answers to a wide range of philosophical questions.

The following questions represent some of the many that Betty has been asked. They concern man's relation to the universe, how he actually grows to know God, the nature of God, how spirit guides fit into all of this, and the like. There is much more to be explored. Betty looks forward to continuing such questioning in the months and years ahead.

HOW WOULD YOU EXPLAIN "GOD"?

God is a dynamic force, a power, the creator. He masterminded the plan of the universe, and it is He alone who has the power to give life.

He is the ultimate and the infinite. But what human mind can understand such things?

Imagine an atomic power plant operated by thousands of persons, with hundreds of thousands of computer circuits, all attached to an *intellect*. This intellect knows where everything belongs at all times, and can see how everything will unfold and develop. This will give you not even a tiny glimpse of what God is like.

God is benevolent, he is loving, and he is also just. This means he knows and cares about every creature—not that one should be free from everything that might hurt, but that what is for one's best good in the long run might be attained. His justice means that each person receives the result of what he does, for it is only in this way that people learn the lessons that lead them closer to the God-plan and the God-nature. Even though painful, the divine justice is really an aspect of the divine goodness.

YOU SPEAK OF GOD AS "HE."

God is universal energy and has no gender. "He" is more Betty's concept than ours. Other traditions may refer to God as "she" or "it." Don't get hung-up on things like this. Do you think God cares what pronoun you use?

WHAT ABOUT THE PERSON WHO REGARDS
HIMSELF AS AN ATHEIST?

An atheist is an entity which has turned
away from religious dogma and ritual. Usually
atheists are people who are disillusioned by those
who give lip service to religion, or go through
its outward forms, but do not practice it toward
their fellow men. Or they've been taught ideas
about God they just can't swallow.

For the most part atheists are honest seekers
who are on the threshold of fuller insight. Their
main problem is that they usually try to understand God with the intellect alone. And they
are too quick to say "there is no God" based
on the hypocrisy they see among various religious groups.

But it is often better to be a sincere atheist
than a hypocrital or bigoted religious person.
Almost every atheist is ready to grant there is
a higher power, or energy, or process, operative
in the universe. But he doesn't want to call
this power God because of the negative conno-
tations he has for the word   God.

SOMETIMES YOU SPEAK OF THIS
WORLD AS A PLACE OF   ILLUSION.
WHAT DOES THIS MEAN?

With your physical senses you quite naturally
see the world as a conglomeration of separate

things. Pretend you are looking at an apple and a stone sitting side by side. They appear separate and different. But what are they *really*? Each is a manifestation of *energy*. Your physicists describe the make-up of things in terms of protons, neutrons, and electrons—which in turn form atoms. These atoms are energy fields, and they make up "different" substances because of differing vibrational rates. In other words, both the apple and the stone are manifestations of energy with varying rates of vibration. And if you could *see* these vibrations, you would see that they extend outward and intermingle. At some point the stone and the apple blend into one another on a *continuum* of energy. If you could see into their true nature, you would know them to be only differing expressions of the same basic reality.

Your notion of separateness prevents you from understanding the universal, all-encompassing creative force. Your intellect or rational mind depends on your sense organs for information. These are valuable tools for man, but tools of limited usefulness. Both the senses and the rational mind are primitive levels of consciousness.

Can the intellect grasp "infinity"? Can the rational mind understand the energy which is the essence of life—when at this point you cannot see or measure that force? You will never be able to integrate the concept of the God-force into the part of your being that is a prisoner of the five senses.

The illusion of the earth plane is a problem only because you are not on a vibrational attunement that enables you to see the reality behind the outer appearances. The word illusion does not mean that the earth plane is imaginary or a hallucination—but you do not perceive it as it *really is*. And how you perceive it depends on the development of your own consciousness.

FROM TIME TO TIME BETTY'S MESSAGE
DEALS WITH "GUARDIAN ANGELS" AND
"HELPING ENTITIES" IN THE SPIRIT REALMS.
HOW DO THESE RELATE TO GOD?

You have no idea how full your universe is of waves and rays, forces and entities! But again, you have limited physical equipment for experiencing these while you are in an earthly body. Only now are some of your scientists learning to measure energy fields which are independent of the vibrations you call the material world.

Young people today talk about good vibes and bad vibes. They are learning to sense the subtler aspects of their world. The spiritual masters of all religions always have been highly sensitive to the presence of forces or powers around them. But how were they to describe them to others who couldn't see or feel these presences?

Empty space is full! Each of you is surrounded by beings, spirits, entities—call them what you wish. They possess the characteristics you call consciousness and intelligence. And they are as real as anything you perceive in the physical world. On ocassion they take on a rate of vibration (or you raise your own) that lets you see them with your eyes and hear them with your ears. But normally, if you are aware of them at all, it is through feeling a presence, through thought, or mental pictures. You may, of course, speak to them out loud, but they hear your thoughts as readily as they hear your words.

What are these beings? There are all kinds, just as there are all kinds of people. We would describe them as having differing vibrational levels. The lower levels are the less well-developed; the higher levels are the more spiritually advanced. You attract to yourself those which are compatible with your own level of development. Another way to explain it is that God gives you those whom you need to help you further your development at your particular level of growth.

These spirit guides are your teachers. And in order to be a spirit guide they must know more, or be more advanced, than you are yourself. They lead you into and through the experiences you need to live out your karma. They have various personalities and you may get to know them by their sense of humor, their playfulness, or their sternness. You may even be given a name to call them. But they will change from time to time, and you may find yourself with completely new guides.

Only your *guardian angel* is assigned to you at birth and stays with you throughout your entire incarnation. It is "his" job—of course, "he" has no gender—to keep a record of your growth, your positive and negative karma, and to give you the karma you've chosen to work out in your present existence.

The most important thing about these helping entities is that *they love you*. Their present task is *to help you grow*! They are expressions of the divine love.

You are never alone. You are surrounded constantly by loving, caring beings who will never violate your freedom or impose themselves upon you. But they will assist, prod, and prompt you as you permit. Meditation is the special time for you to attune yourself to them, to open yourself to the insight and guidance they want to bring you.

How are we to understand the nature of our own individual soul or self?

This is man's age-old search: "Who or what am I?" The discovery of what you are is your life task. We can give you an explanation in words. But the knowing of your true nature must ultimately come from within. When you achieve this you will not need words.

You are, in essence, a divine spark, a particular individualized expression of the infinite light, or God. The light which is distinctively *you* takes on an individuality, a personality, in each incarnation.

It is this personality which attracts to you the persons with whom you have karmic ties to be worked out. The personality, individuality, or ego—this is a tool to help you regain your spiritual sight.

As you go through life, you discover more fully who and what you are. You see yourself in a wider and wider perspective. You see that you are a part of the one source of all things, of all existence, of all creatures.

You are all things in all places in all realms, but are limited by the lack of knowledge and ignorance of your own stage of development. The God-consciousness, the I AM, is what you are.

Our counsel is that you not be so concerned with seeking an explanation of self which can be put into words. Rather be concerned with developing the techniques for going to the God-center within. And as thoughts of separateness, of ego, fade away, you will find the nature and purpose of your true being.

HOW IMPORTANT IS THE PHYSICAL BRAIN
IN OUR TOTAL MAKE-UP?

The brain is like a high-powered computer. Add to the brain the spine and endocrine glands and you have a complex interconnected system. It is this system which provides the structure for the energy centers you call the chakras. The entire brain-spine-endocrine system functions as a powerful energy unit.

Ultimately, thought is not dependent on this system even while you are in a bodily incarnation. Through telepathy, soul travel, and the like, the consciousness which is essentially *you* can learn to leave and return to the body at will. But the physical vehicle is the temporary home of the spiritual, and it should be respected and maintained as a healthy dwelling place.

If you knew how to tap and use the energy from this powerful system, you could literally move mountains. The present experiments in psychokinesis are but kindergarten examples of this power.

WHAT ACTUALLY IS CONSCIOUSNESS?

Uvalla is saying that it would be a difficult task to explain through this channel at this time. A year from now, perhaps. But to try to put this complex matter simply, consciousness is that aspect of the individual God-self which has the ability to interpret the vibrations of various levels and planes of being. It interprets the vibrations of matter received through the senses, and translates them into the pictures you see of the real world around you.

MANY PEOPLE SEEM TO BE DISTURBED BY WHAT THEY REGARD AS THEIR SINFULNESS. WHAT IS SIN?

We wish this word could be eliminated from your vocabulary. For sin implies the doing of that which offends God and thus causes him to "punish" you—a total misconception of the love nature of the infinite reality.

Much of what you call sin is failure to follow man-made ethical rules. The law of God is not the same thing as the laws of man. What people consider punishment for sin is really karmic opportunity to learn to reach out in compassion to one's fellows.

Sin is not the making of mistakes. If the word is used at all, it would have to be in the context of "refusing to grow and learn from your mistakes." But in the ultimate scheme of things, this is impossible. Some people may take longer than others, but all will grow.

Rather than dwell upon sin it is best to *concentrate on the positive*—growth in love and compassion. The minister or speaker who continues to stress "the sinfulness of the people" is perpetuating negative vibrations, not creating a feeling of self-love and oneness with the God-force.

Know that God is love and learn to live by the law of love: treat others as you would like to be treated.

WHAT IS "GOD'S WILL," OR THE "COSMIC WILL"?

The cosmic will expresses itself as the God within, or the higher self. It is contrasted with the human will, which all too often rests on selfish desires. The cosmic will is constantly bombarding the entity with truth. Some call this conscience, others the inner voice.

The higher will, prompting toward growth in love, may be listened to or ignored. *But it will always be there.* Normally it operates through helping entities, the spirit guides or teachers.

The human task is to learn to work with the cosmic will, and thus to bring about growth through the choices made in many incarnations. Each person is an individual creation, yet a part of the whole. Through response to the cosmic will one advances toward his true home, his union with the infinite.

YOUR ANSWERS TO ALMOST EVERY QUESTION HAVE SPOKEN OF THE GROWTH OR DEVELOPMENT OF THE SOUL. WILL YOU ELABORATE ON THIS?

It is not difficult to understand that the life processes you see around you involve growth. The seed springs into the tiny blade, the blade into the plant, the plant brings forth flowers— all through an unfolding process in response to the light of the sun.

Man, too, is like a seed. Within him is the potential of the fully conscious being. And his "growth"—in response to the Light—is also a process of *unfolding*. Through this process man is literally becoming as the Light, for he is changing into lighter and finer vibrations.

But man has the ability consciously to direct his unfolding. He may hasten it, by giving himself plenty of spiritual food and water. Or he may slow it down considerably by choosing to grow in rocky soil, or by springing up among the shadows.

From birth to death, through the many lifetimes, the vibrational rate of the entity continues to change, to heighten. Growth in this sense means the heightening of vibrations,

for as you grow in love you are attuning,
or heightening your vibrations, to the powerful
love vibration. Heightening the vibrations means
expanding the awareness.

When man's vibrational rate becomes such
that it is one with the time and space vibration,
then man is no longer limited by these energies.
He blends with and expands through them. His
awareness has grown. When man's vibrational rate becomes such that he blends with the
life beat on other planes, then he is no longer
restricted from experiencing these planes.

When man's vibrations become such that he
can blend with the Light—the highest source—
then he is able to experience the true nature of
his being, to know all things.

▲

It seems that indeed we may ask an abun-
dance of questions. But we do not always receive
ready answers. Perhaps the underlying counsel
of Betty's channel is: *To know you must grow.*
For in growing we are attuning ourselves to
higher and higher levels of vibration, hence
expanding our awareness.

The way to grow seems complex—but
repeatedly its simplicity is stressed. Be still and
listen to the subtler vibrations, the voices, within
you. Be still and attune yourself to the powerful

energy forces within. Be still, through your daily practice of meditation, and you will learn to know the purpose and Source of your being...

You will learn to know the "I AM" of the universe.